Shaking the Dust:
Stepping from Darkness into
LIGHT

K. A. Merkel

WESTBOW®
PRESS
A DIVISION OF THOMAS NELSON
& ZONDERVAN

Unless otherwise noted, Scripture quotations used in this book are from:
New American Standard Bible, Creation House, Inc., Carol Stream, Illinois,
The Lockman Foundation 1960, 1962, 1963, 1971, 1973, 1975, 1977

Author Credits: Bachelors of Arts – Fine Arts and Art History, University of
Northern Colorado, Greeley, Colorado and Masters of Christian
Education – Youth Ministry, Bethel Theological Seminary, Saint Paul, Minnesota

WestBow Press books may be ordered through booksellers or by contacting:

WestBow Press
A Division of Thomas Nelson & Zondervan
1663 Liberty Drive
Bloomington, IN 47403
www.westbowpress.com
1 (866) 928-1240

Because of the dynamic nature of the Internet, any web addresses or
links contained in this book may have changed since publication and
may no longer be valid. The views expressed in this work are solely those
of the author and do not necessarily reflect the views of the publisher,
and the publisher hereby disclaims any responsibility for them.

Photography by - K. A. Merkel - Cover Photo: Polar bear sniffing tundra
buggy tracks on the Hudson Bay, Churchill, Manitoba, Canada.

ISBN: 978-1-4908-3895-3 (sc)
ISBN: 978-1-4908-3896-0 (hc)
ISBN: 978-1-4908-3894-6 (e)

Library of Congress Control Number: 2014909659

Printed in the United States of America.

WestBow Press rev. date: 06/10/2014

Contents

Preface

Throughout your life journey, many things will influence its path. God's extravagant and amazing mercy, grace, and love will surround you each new day and as you yield your life to Him. By trusting in Him, you will be restored and refreshed, and you will be defined by His power and glory!

Just as the polar bear needs to adapt to its ever-changing circumstances and threats to its environment, so will you on your life's journey. You have come or will go through life with some "battle scars across your nose" as well. And as you sniff out the changing circumstances and environment that have overtaken you, you must find renewed focus and purpose, or you will become extinct in this life, which you have been called to live by your Creator God. Your world as well is impacted by climate change (physical, social, emotional, spiritual, and mental) and humankind's impact on your life. This world seeks to hold you securely away from a vibrant relationship with your Everlasting Father and from the heart of God. Praise the Lord God Almighty, who sent His Son, Jesus Christ, to walk on earth and die on the cross for your sins. Praise God that the Lord Jesus Christ was raised from the dead, forever transforming your sinful nature. You have been forever changed and are hidden at the cross in the shed blood of the Lord Jesus Christ for all eternity. As His child, you can live defined by His mercy, grace, and love and be surrounded by His light and peace.

This book is dedicated to my brothers and sisters in Christ, who have come alongside and walked this life journey with me, and to the all the saints who have journeyed before us. May we continue to proclaim the good news of the Risen Jesus Christ and His power to restore and change individuals. To Him be all glory, power, and dominion forever … Amen!

 **1**　*Our Journey into the Light*

The fall of 2012 found me embarking on a journey that my friend defined as one from darkness into light. As I boarded the Canadian Railroad train departing for Churchill, Manitoba and the shores of the Hudson Bay to observe polar bears in their natural environment, I didn't know what to expect. Our tour group was a mix of individuals from all walks of life, all ages, and from the United States and Europe. Our common bond was a love for the polar bear and a new adventure.

By the end of the first day of our two-day train journey to Churchill, all known civilization had faded away with each passing mile: no roads, no cars or trucks, no phones, no Internet, no major chain stores, and no fast-food restaurants. We found ourselves wrapped in the cold and silence of the snow and the rhythmic rocking of the train as it clanked on the rails, moving us further into the subarctic of Canada. Our polar journey had become timeless.

We wondered how the residents of the few, sparsely populated communities we passed through survived. What did these individuals do for a living? How did they handle the harsh climate and all that comes with living in the subarctic? Things we're convinced are "must haves," to exist, for the most part, weren't a part of their lifestyle. By observing the harshness of the land and listening to the silence of their world, we could feel their strength and determination to persevere regardless of what the day brought forth. Many of the people we met shaped their circumstances and environment; they didn't allow their circumstances or the subarctic environment shape and control them. They were gracious, generous, and happy individuals. Their determination brought forth dependence on one another that rested in their faith.

At one stop I assumed the train would pull straight out of the station and continue our journey north. However, the train backed up for what seemed like an eternity. This caused me to reflect on my life, especially where I had been during the past year, and how I felt like I was completely on the wrong track. My mother had recently passed from complications of dementia and I had lost my dream job. (or was it really?) Sitting on that train, I thought, Man, this train ride is like my life; it's going backward, and this makes no sense!

In the silence of that moment, God reminded me that even though I felt like I was going backward with my life and goals, I was really going forward in His plan for my life. His plan would take care of the seemingly backward motion and enable me to reach the destination and plan He holds close to His heart for me. With dependence, continual prayer, and trust, I needed to listen and cling to His hope that was rising on the cold horizon. I needed to listen for the sound of His strong, still whisper in the silence that engulfed me. In the stillness that approached on the horizon, I would hear God whisper when I stopped, waited, and listened. It was my choice how I would handle my circumstances and environment. Would I allow God to lead and define me and my future, or would I allow my circumstances and environment to define and control me? God was presenting me with a new beginning. He was rearranging my known past and securities by taking the residue from recent dust storms found in lost dreams and unmet goals and moving me to a new horizon. I didn't want the negativity and icy dust of confusion, uncertainty, anxiety, bitterness, and so on, to define my life. I am a child of the Lord God Almighty, and I want to be defined by His amazing grace, love, and mercy. He has a plan for me, and I choose to walk in it.

The train eventually returned to the main track, and we began heading north, toward Churchill. And not long after my trip, God would provide me with a new job and restored joy, which is found in clinging to Jesus' side as I walk this earthly journey one day at a time, moment by moment.

That same evening, as we continued toward the ebony blackness, the northern lights formed a delicate and huge crystalline-white arch of what looked like glitter across the northern sky. The stars and planets were extremely brilliant in the deep black sky. The light of the arch reminded me of the pure light of God and His provision for me—and you—in Jesus Christ. The crystal arch became a symbol for me of my ongoing life journey to draw closer to God's amazing love, provision, and daily blessings. It made me long for heaven's shores and the eternal gates of heaven. As I rested in the silence, I found my heart praising God for who He was, is, and will ever be.

Worthy is the Lamb that was slain to receive power and the riches and wisdom and might and honor and glory and blessing." And every created thing which is in heaven and on the earth and under the earth and on the sea, and all things in them, I heard saying, "To Him who sits on the throne, and to the Lamb, be blessing and honor and glory and dominion forever and ever ... Amen." (Revelation 5:12–14)

A Lesson from the Lord of the Artic—aka, the Polar Bear Vulnerability—James 4:10

As my time in Churchill came to a close and I reflected on my new friend, the polar bear reminded me of the many lessons God uses to teach me about how I, too, should approach my life journey.

> Speak when necessary.
> Be majestic.
> Be inquisitive, strong, and perserver.
> Sniff out what the day has in store.
> Be at peace with what the day brings my way.

2 On the Mountaintop - The Canyon of Shadows

O Lord, Thou hast searched me and known me. Thou dost know when I sit down and when I rise up; Thou dost understand my thought from afar. Thou dost scrutinize my path and my laying down, And art intimately acquainted with all of my ways. Even before there is a word on my tongue, Behold, O Lord, Thou dost know it all. Thou hast enclosed me behind and before, And laid Thy hand upon me.

—Psalm 139:1–5

In most discussions about the ups and downs of life, you will come across family members or friends who talk about mountaintop experiences, valleys, and what I call, the canyons of our life journeys. The mountaintop experiences are the "wow" moments of life, where everything exceeds our dreams and expectations. If you have had the opportunity to be on top of a mountain at the continental divide, or even at a mountain overlook, the vantage point and grandeur of the views are breathtaking. Most people would love to linger there as long as possible, especially since "wow" moments such as these seem to be over far too quickly.

The valleys are where most of us live and walk on a daily basis. And like most valleys, there are sunny spots and shadows along the journey that enhance or detract from the scenery. The canyons are those darker places that end up stretching your character and define who you are. If you have visited the Grand Canyon, you know the canyon walls are steep and the shadows dark. But occasionally, even on the canyon floor, there are glimmers and rays of sunlight. It is a long way to the top from the canyon floor. To climb the trail to the crest of the canyon is a daunting, challenging task. The trail you climb in your life journey can be the same. There are awesome moments, such as the birth of a child, set alongside the death of a parent. Then there are the daily routines that bring you comfort and joy, and times when you feel worn, tired, and in need of something, or someone, to strengthen, guide, or carry you to the top of the crest of the canyon.

God is present in all these life moments. Through the power of His Holy Spirit and in His Son, Jesus Christ, He will restore and help you through all your life moments. You must include Christ in every detail of your life, trusting that He is there and will be your Guide and Comforter along the journey, whether the trail is level, high, and steep, or closer to the canyon floor. One of my favorite quotes is, "God is more concerned about my character than my circumstances." (unknown) It is in the defining moments of life that you learn of God's love, power, mercy, grace, comfort, and peace in an all-embracing manner. God, the Creator, is fully acquainted with everything about you. He knew you when you were being formed in your mother's womb. He knows every breath that you take, every thought that you think or word that you speak. He loves you through the good and bad times of your life. He will never leave you or forsake you! He will always be close by to listen, rescue, and guide you. All you need to do is ask Him for help. His grace is amazing, and His love for you is extravagant.

For Thou didst form my inward parts; Thou didst weave me in my mother's womb. I will give thanks to Thee, for I am fearfully and wonderfully made; Wonderful are Thy works, And my soul knows it very well. (Psalm 139:13–14)

"For I know the plans that I have for you," declares the Lord, "plans for welfare and not for calamity to give you a future and a hope. Then you will call upon Me and come and pray to Me, and I will listen to you. And you will seek Me and find Me, when you search for Me with all your heart. And I will be found by you," declares the Lord ... (Jeremiah 29:11–14)

Your character and priorities fall in line with what you consider to be important in your life. Your character is established by your core values and the belief system you hold close to your heart. As a result, your character and priorities define who you are. If you haven't acknowledged Jesus Christ as your Lord and Savior and if you don't allow Him to be a priority and of utmost importance in your life, you will not be open and eager to pursuing godly character and other-centered priorities.

Walking with Christ as your Lord and Savior is a lifelong endeavor. Is He in your life and central in all your choices, priorities, and goals? Or is God "somewhat present" but not really included in your life? If you keep Christ at arm's length and don't allow Him to truly be involved—to fill His rightful place at the center of your life—your journey will fall short of all God has intended for you.

What do you allow to define who you are? Are you defined by the world's standards and come up empty-handed at the end of the day? Take a moment, and reflect on your life and the choices that define who you are. What role do you allow Jesus Christ to have in your life? Is He residing with you and directing your life choices, priorities, and goals? Or is He outside, at an arm's length, because you know what is best for your life, and He will just mess things up?

If you are unsure that Jesus Christ has a central place in your life, you can pray a simple prayer such as,

> Lord Jesus, I have fallen short and have sinned against You. I ask Your forgiveness for every wrong action or attitude I have had. Thank You for Your death on the cross and for restoring me to a right relationship with You. Please be a part of my life, and walk with me each day. Teach and help me to seek You in the good and the hard times of my life. Thank You for hearing my prayer. Amen.

Living the Christian life and seeking to follow Jesus Christ, apart from allowing the power of the Holy Spirit to lead and guide you, is like having a lamp and not plugging it into the outlet so it can receive the power required to light up the room. By not allowing God's Holy Spirit to lead you on a moment-by-moment basis, you will become frustrated, weary, and tired as you travel this life journey. The canyons, valleys, and mountaintop experiences will soon begin to define you, instead of you defining the circumstances and environment that have overtaken you. The storms of life are hard; the wind and the waves can become very high and overwhelming. By keeping your focus on Jesus Christ, by asking Him for help each moment of every day, by acknowledging His blessing each day (big or small, His blessings are there; watch for them!), your circumstances and environment will not define who you are. Jesus Christ will define who you are. You are His child, a child of the Lord God Almighty, your Heavenly Father!

And in the fourth watch of the night He came to them, walking on the sea. And when the disciples saw Him walking on the sea, they were frightened, saying, "It is a ghost!" And they cried out for fear. But immediately Jesus spoke to them, saying, "Take courage, it is I; do not be afraid." And Peter answered Him and said, "Lord if it is You, command me to come to You on the water." And He said, "Come!" And Peter got out of the boat, and walked on the water and came toward Jesus. But seeing the wind, he became afraid, and beginning to sink, he cried out saying, "Lord, save me!" And immediately Jesus stretched out His hand and took hold of him, and said to him, "O you of little faith, why did you doubt?" (Matthew 14:25–31)

When you feel like you are sinking in the storms of your life, reach out and take Jesus Christ's hand. Whatever your battle, if you take your eyes off the Lord Jesus Christ, you will sink in your own efforts and selfish orientations. This will defeat you faster than any other tool Satan may toss your way. Run fast in the opposite direction, and seek shelter in the arms of the Most High God! God will provide for your needs. When Peter began to sink in the rising waters around him, he focused on Jesus Christ and reached out and took hold of Christ's hand. He looked for God's blessing instead of allowing the troubled waters of his past or present circumstances to define how his life journey would be viewed.

Therefore, since we have so great a cloud of witnesses surrounding us, let us also lay aside every encumbrance, and the sin which so easily entangles us, and let us run with endurance the race that is set before us, fixing our eyes on Jesus, the author and perfecter of faith, who for the joy set before Him endured the cross, despising the shame, and has sat down at the right hand of the throne of God. For consider Him ... (Hebrews 12:1–3a)

The Lord's lovingkindnesses indeed never cease, For His compassions never fail. They are new every morning; Great is Thy faithfulness. (Lamentations 3:22–23)

Through the ages, men and women of faith have lived amid their worn and broken circumstances and surroundings. God has moved many individuals beyond the weary and broken pieces of their lives and on to a new horizon or beginning. All have acquired a strengthened heart for God; all have at some point turned to their Redeemer God with a humbled heart and a spirit of thankfulness based on gratitude. All have been shakers of the dust that could have encased them. And they left the dust of the broken pieces of their lives at the foot of the cross of Christ. Their focus has been on the Risen Christ and how He can be glorified though their less-than-favorable life circumstances. Their lives serve as examples for us today.

Many men and women of faith have their life journeys documented for us in God's Word, the Bible. Men and women, individuals like you and me, stood strong, empowered by the Holy Spirit and the love of Jesus Christ to make a difference on this journey called life. How were they able to shake off the dust, those broken pieces that could have left them weary, tired, and downtrodden? How were they able to rise above those moments in life when the going got tough? How did they know when and where to shake off the dust of the negative choices that could have encumbered and sadly defined their character for the rest of their life journey? How did they know when to stay or when to move on at the bidding of their Everlasting Father? How did they graciously and effectively live through the storms of life when the raging sea didn't calm down around them?

Let's look at several men and women of faith and observe, study, and reflect on their trust, hope, faith, and obedience in Jesus Christ to discover how their daily choices built their character and strengthened them to remain secure in their commitment and worship of the Father, Son, and Holy Spirit. Here's to shaking the dust and the icy darkness in our own lives so the worn and broken pieces can fall off and His light can shine brilliantly on the hillside for all to see the glory of the Risen Lord and Savior Jesus Christ, whom we love and serve on this earthly journey called life.

> *You are the light of the world. A city set on a hill cannot be hidden. Nor do men light a lamp, and put it under the peck-measure, but on the lampstand; and it gives light to all who are at home. Let your light so shine before men in such a way that they may see your good works, and glorify your Father who is in heaven. (Matthew 5:14–16)*

How are you defined?

I am defined by the love and grace of my Creator God, who is made known to me through the power of the Holy Spirit, found only in Jesus Christ, who is God's only Son and my Savior and Lord.

A Lesson from a Polar Bear
Confidence—Proverbs 14:26
Whisker Spots and Fingerprints

You are fearfully and wonderfully made, and God loves and knows every inch of your person. Never doubt for a minute that He isn't intimately involved in who you are and who you are becoming! A research project (2012 and 2013) in Churchill, Manitoba, Canada, through the Churchill Northern Studies Center, identified polar bears by their unique whisker spots and facial scarring. These markings are used much like law enforcement officers use fingerprints to identify human beings. This polar bear research is allowing scientists to identify one polar bear from another, from year to year, as they migrate to the sea ice. This also enables them to determine the polar bear's movement throughout the subarctic region. Since God has given so much attention to detail with one of His animal creatures, how much more concentrated attention does He lavish on you? No polar bear has the same whisker spots. No other person ever created has your fingerprints. Know that your Creator God cares intimately for you. He is forever forgiving, forever loving, forever looking, and forever wanting you to come to Him.

3 Shaking the Dust of Weariness, Fatigue, and Regret - Defined by Purpose and Restored Joy

But thanks be to God, who always leads us in His triumph in Christ, and manifests through us the sweet aroma of the knowledge of Him in every place. For we are a fragrance of Christ to God among those who are being saved and among those who are perishing.

—*2 Corinthians 2:14–15*

As human beings, there are those moments in life when, if you are honest, you feel weary, fatigued, rejected, or broken inside. You are unsure how the future will unfold for you, your family, for a friend, or maybe for someone you have heard about but don't know personally. You may be tempted to run away—physically, socially, emotionally, spiritually, and/or mentally. You have probably heard the phrase, "Bad things happen to good people," or, "That just doesn't make sense." At some point, all of us are likely to feel that this is a circumstance we have encountered or are currently experiencing. How can you shake off the dust, the broken pieces of whatever it is that has worn you out, discouraged and crushed your heart and left you shattered in a thousand pieces?

You need and want to shake off the dust of the moment/day/year—but how? There is no energy left—where do you turn? Life has become overwhelming, unfair, frightening, and/or may seem out of control. The dust may seem more like ice crystals, and you find the darkness of winter creeping in on top of you while you are surrounded in the heat of the moment! Your darkness has swallowed you and left you full of fear and anxiety. You have tried looking up but finding hope either seems futile or too far away. Maybe in the midst of your brokenness, hope, strength, and trust really just seem a prayer away, or maybe you feel that you are caught somewhere in between, hanging by your fingertips.

One doesn't have to look very far to see how restless humankind has become. Many individuals appear not to have an interest in spiritual things or an interest in changing the choices they make daily. However, the world we live in desperately seeks Jesus Christ. Many of those we know and come in contact with each day are searching in the wrong places. To acknowledge the world and see those around us as Jesus does, through a heart of love and compassion, is something that, as Christians, we all need to ask the Holy Spirit to build into our lives. The human heart is restless until it finds balance, purpose, security, and peace in Jesus Christ.

Remember, in this lifetime and the next, you will reap what you sow based on how your life is defined and lived. God's Holy Spirit will build in you the character qualities that define you as God's child. Choose to walk a new life that is secure and defined by Jesus Christ. It would be better to sow a life that demonstrates the following attitudes and behaviors: God-fearing, purity, honorable, holy, honest, at peace, moral, committed, supportive, passionate, ethically sound, and respectful. Many who live by the world's standards find themselves following after the lust of the flesh (pleasure), lust of the eyes (prosperity), and the boastful pride of life (power). Pleasure, prosperity, and/or power have become their god(s) (1 John 2:16–17). Some of the attitudes and behaviors that demonstrate and define someone who lives by any combination of the three sinful desires mentioned in 1 John 2:16-17 are exhibiting inappropriate behaviors, are irreconcilable, disrespectful, boastful, using bad language, self-serving, conceited, without self-control, arrogant, malicious gossips, ignorant, and being mockers of others (known and unknown). Shaking the dust of behaviors and attitudes that define you by the world's standards and seeking to follow your Creator God's path for you will result in a life being defined by integrity and morality, accountability and discipline, obedience and self-control, respect and honor, passion and conviction. Jesus is daily taking your dust and broken pieces (circumstances) and is (and has) made you complete. He has defined who you are in Him. You are loved, safe, and secure in Him regardless of what the world throws your way or how it makes you feel. God is ever present and He has a purpose for you. He is watching over everything that concerns you.

Do not be deceived, God is not mocked; for whatever a man sows, this he will also reap. (Galatians 6:7)

We are all sinful, fall short of the glory of God, and are separated from God (Romans 3:23; 6:23). It is only by God's grace and His mercy that we can turn to Him and receive His free gift of salvation through Jesus Christ (Ephesians 2:8–9). Do you, or the individuals you come in contact with each day, have a living relationship with the God who created you? This living relationship is found in God's only Son, Jesus Christ. John 3:16 states, "For God so loved the world, that He gave His only begotten Son, that whoever believes in Him should not perish, but have everlasting life." By acknowledging and accepting Jesus Christ as your Lord and Savior, the patterns of making choices that inappropriately define who you are will be changed forever! To begin a living and personal relationship with Jesus Christ, all you need to do is to turn from your selfish desires, and trust Him to come into your life to forgive your sins and make you the person He created you to be. Through prayer (talking openly and honestly with God) and by seeking and turning your life over to Him, you become His child, and you are no longer defined by the world's standards or your past choices. You are defined by God's great love, His amazing grace, and His mercy as you trust Him each day, moment by moment. You are forgiven! You are loved! You are healed in Him!

> Thou hast made us for Thyself O God, and our hearts are restless until they find their rest in Thee. (Saint Augustine, philosopher, AD 354–AD 430)

> There is a God-shaped vacuum in the heart of every man which cannot be satisfied by any created thing, but only by God, the Creator, made known through Jesus Christ. (Pascal, French physicist and philosopher, AD 1623–AD 1662)

In Matthew 28:18–20 and Acts 1:8, Jesus Christ extends to His disciples the call of the Great Commission: "you shall receive power when the Holy Spirit has come upon you; and you shall be My witnesses both in Jerusalem, and in all Judea and Samaria, and even to the remotest part of the earth." Saint Francis of Assisi (AD 1182–AD 1226), a prophet and founder of the Franciscan Order, taught that we need to go and share the gospel of Jesus Christ, and use words if necessary. You are called to go and be the sweet fragrance of Jesus Christ (2 Corinthians 2:14–15) in a world that is struggling and seeking purpose and fulfillment in life. Many are weary, tired, discouraged, and/or broken inside— just like you. What are you doing to make wiser choices for your own life? What are you doing to help the world around you make wiser choices? The wisest choice of all is to know Jesus Christ, the Son of God, as Lord and Savior and to live a life that is empowered by His Holy Spirit and filled with love and purpose.

The conclusion, when all has been heard, is: fear God and keep His commandments, because this applies to every person. Because God will bring every act to judgment, everything which is hidden, whether it is good or evil. (Ecclesiastes 12:13–14)

As you walk this life journey, many will be open to Christ's message, and some will not. The thought of Jesus' words to His disciples to go and share what you have seen and heard and if you aren't received shake the dust off your feet as you leave and your peace will return to you, often comes to mind (Matthew 10:5–15; Acts 13:51). When do you know it is time to shake off the dusty, icy darkness of heart that has come over you due to your circumstances? And what is it you are really shaking off?

Shaking the dust can focus on shaking off an attitude of heart—such as bitterness, anger, regret, deceit, disappointment, and discouragement—in order that you may experience joy and peace in this life journey. It means making a choice to leave the bad attitude, the disappointment, the death of a vision/dream, the death of a loved one, financial woes, broken relationships, or … *fill in the* blank … behind. It means not letting these attitudes take possession of your thoughts, your heart, soul, and character. These attitudes, thoughts, and feelings may be directed toward others or toward yourself. In leaving a worn spot in my life, I did physically shake off the dust from my feet. However, the frustration, confusion, tears, and anger I had begun to feel were shaken off as well. Throughout my life journey, God rescues me as I keep my focus on Him daily, moment by moment. He protects me in the rising stormy waters and fire and moves me to place of peace and joy as I rest in the palm of His powerful and almighty hand, close to His heart! Just like the dust that accumulates in your home, once it is removed, things shine, look restored, and brand new. So it is with shaking the dust of bitterness, anger, regret, deceit, disappointment, discouragement, and so on, from your life. In allowing God's forgiveness to restore you, you will be set free to forgive and move on in your life journey, and you will be defined by God, who faithfully provides for and loves you beyond measure. Walk in the power of the Holy Spirit, and allow Jesus Christ to dust you off and revive your strength of heart and soul.

How do your choices impact and define your life? How do your choices impact the lives of others around you? When I have felt worn and broken, I didn't want to become bitter and angry. I wanted my light to shine as a child of Jesus Christ. I wanted to demonstrate through my actions and words what it meant to walk in the power of His Holy Spirit and in the mercy of God's grace and love each day. I needed to let the past and present fall away and move toward the light of His love, mercy, and grace. I needed to live where He planted me. I needed my choices to reflect His character and love in and through me. My choices in the stormy waters and fire would impact the rest of my life and those around me. Walking closely with Jesus Christ doesn't mean life will be a bed of roses. Remember that even a rose has a thorny stem. However, the gardener tenderly cares for the soil and the conditions the rose requires to become the fragrant flower he created it to be. By living your life according to godly principles, you will stand apart just by the nature of what defines your life journey.

There are times in life when God calls us to live and move in a circumstance that isn't easy. There are times in life when the difficult time is for a season, and in His perfect timing, He moves us out of those deep canyons of shadows and darkness. Trusting in His care, guiding hand, and His perfect plan for you allows you to continue to the high places of your life, whether you are moved out of those canyons or if you continue to walk through them, relying on His faithfulness and mercy. Know that regardless of the circumstance or surroundings, He is walking with you and will never leave or forsake you. When you can't sense His presence that is when He is the closest, holding and supporting you in the darkness of the canyon floor.

As a believer in Christ, you are called to serve Him wherever you are. Whatever vocation God has called you to, you are also called to be in relationship and connectedness with others. You are called to serve and make a difference in the world around you by loving others through a listening ear and prayer, through lending a helping hand, providing clothing, a meal, a ride, and so on. Being His light, His sweet fragrance, and an example to those you come in contact with each day by rejoicing in their blessings and helping to bear their burdens is a privilege. How you walk your life journey with family, friends, and those God brings across your path each day defines who you are. Whether you are attending school, work at home, are retired, or have a job outside the home, God has called you to be His light in the world. How you respond to the world and those in your sphere of influence, and how you respond to Christ's leading in your life, determines how your character will be defined and grow.

Jonah's Journey

And He said to him, "You shall love the Lord your God with all your heart, and with all your soul and with all your mind." This is the great and foremost commandment. The second is like it, "You shall love your neighbor as yourself." (Matthew 22:37–39)

The word of the Lord came to Jonah the son of Amittai saying, "Arise, go …" (Jonah 1:1–2a)

Jonah, a prophet to Israel, lived during the eighth century BC. Many biblical scholars recognize Jonah as the first missionary. If you have ever known anyone who has been called to serve on the mission field (developing nation or at home), you can observe that his or her life is passionately called to serve and make a difference in the unique sphere of influence where God has planted the person. This same passion should be a part of your daily life as you serve the Lord where He has planted you. You, too, are God's missionary to those around you each day. He will use you to bring His message of love and redemption to a world longing for purpose and fulfillment.

Jonah Chapter 1

Jonah was such a man. He had a heart and passion for the matters of God. He knew God had given him a special call for the nation of Israel. One day God asked Jonah to go to Nineveh and tell them they needed to repent, turn from their evil ways, and seek the Most High and Holy God. And what did Jonah do? He made a 180-degree turn and ran, not walked, to get as far away as possible from God's call and the message he was asked to share with the people of Nineveh. He hurriedly departed. He most likely packed a small bag for his journey, proceeded to the seaport and bought a ticket for Tarshish, got on the boat, went below deck, and quickly fell fast asleep. After all, he had to hurry to accomplish the task God had set before him. Right? Not! As the ship sailed on to its appointed destination, the crew (and napping Jonah) eventually found themselves in the middle of the sea, rocking and rolling. The crew was struggling to save the boat, the cargo, and the passengers. They finally decided to cast lots to see why they were sinking fast in the stormy seas. The lot that was cast fell upon Jonah. When confronted, Jonah confessed he was running from the Lord God and the message of repentance he had been given to share with the citizens of Nineveh. Long story short, the crew tossed Jonah off the boat. However, God wasn't going to give up on Jonah and his decision to avoid this special task. As a result, God provided a big fish that swallowed Jonah to keep him safe and to remind him of God's unfailing love, mercy, and grace. Once Jonah was thrown off the boat, the wind ceased, and the seas became calm. The crew immediately acknowledged, blessed, and praised God for His saving grace.

In reflecting on this part of Jonah's life journey, he truly was on a sinking ship. Have you ever tried to run from God? Why were you running? What were you running from? What was the outcome of your thoughts and actions? How did God lead and protect you during this difficult time? Jonah's choices not only impacted his own life but the lives of those around him. Do you feel like your ship is sinking? Are the storm waters rising quickly? Know that like Jonah, the Lord Jesus Christ will provide for you in your storm. He hasn't deserted you. He holds you securely and safely in the palm of His all-powerful hand.

Jonah Chapters 2–3

The big fish eventually delivered Jonah to land and spit him out. God again asked Jonah to take His message to Nineveh. This time Jonah went directly to Nineveh and shared the message of repentance and deliverance that God asked him to share. When the people heard and received God's message, they humbled their hearts, repented from their sins, and acknowledged God as the Most High and Sovereign King. As a result, God spared the destruction He promised to bring upon their nation.

Jonah Chapter 4

Now after going through a rather dramatic experience of being transported in a big fish and taking the message of repentance and salvation to a nation that didn't have a relationship with God, you would think Jonah, the missionary, would have been very happy for the people of Nineveh: task accomplished, message shared and received with open ears and hearts, and the outcome was good. People's lives were spared, and God's provision was acknowledged. They worshipped the Almighty God. Jonah's response was less than noble. He became very disappointed in God's extravagant love for the people of Nineveh; he became extremely weary, fatigued, and he regretted (was depressed?) that he had ever gone to Nineveh. One can only wonder if Jonah didn't like the fact good things do happen for people who have had a rough go in life. Did Jonah want the praise and recognition that rightfully belonged to the Lord his God? Or maybe Jonah was just angry at or with God? Do you value what resides in the heart of God? Did Jonah value the people he was sent to help? How do your circumstances impact your perspective on life and those around you? Have you ever reacted like Jonah did? What were the results?

Regardless of the storm in your life, God will carry you safely through the raging waters. You are safe in His almighty and powerful arms, because He is faithful. God's love never gives up on you! God knew Jonah better than Jonah knew himself. So as Jonah pouted, God allowed a plant to grow to provide additional shelter and shade to help restore his physical strength and to remind him He still cared about every detail (big or small) in Jonah's life. Jonah was very happy about "his" plant. However, God appointed a worm to come and eat the plant. It withered, and the east winds made the hot sun beat down on Jonah. Jonah was miserable with his circumstance and begged his Heavenly Father to allow him to die. God's questions to Jonah revolved around the plant He had allowed to grow to shelter him from the circumstance of his life journey. "Then the Lord said, 'You had compassion on the plant for which you did not work, and which you did not cause to grow, which came up overnight and perished overnight. And should I not have compassion on Nineveh, the great city in which there are more than 120,000 persons who do not know the difference between their right and left hand, as well as many animals?'" (Jonah 4:10–11).

The storms of your life can be self-inflicted or caused by something or someone outside your control. Regardless of the source of the storm, wind, rain, fire, and turbulence, these circumstances may cause discomfort and pain not only for you but for others. It is okay to express your frustrations, thoughts, feelings, anger, and so on to God. He listens and cares about every detail of your life. Know that God is in control, and His promises don't return empty. He will accomplish His purpose for you, and all things will work together for good.

And we know that God causes all things to work together for good to those who love God, to those who are called according to His purpose. (Romans 8:28)

There are many Scriptures that will confirm for you God's extravagant love and detailed care for all His creation. Jonah saw God's extravagant love and care directed toward the people of Nineveh. Jonah saw God's extravagant love for him through his rescue by the fish while out at sea. God will move heaven and earth to rescue you. There is no place where He can't find you and handle whatever your storm in life might be. You are most precious to Him, and you are created in His image. "And God created man in His own image, in the image of God He created him; male and female" (Genesis 1:27). He provides for you even in your sleep; He knows what you need and when you need it. Seek Him, pray, trust, hope, and rest in His provision and grace.

As you hold forth the light of the gospel of Jesus Christ to those in your unique sphere of influence, God will use your availability to help repair the broken pieces of the hearts of those around you. The Great Shepherd, the Lord Jesus Christ, will be faithful to work His restoration in the lives of others through His Holy Spirit and His shed blood on the cross at Calvary. Are you or a friend battered, bruised, and broken by being tossed around in the storms of life? Pray and humble yourself before the throne of grace, and God will rescue you. He will show you what choices you need to make and what action you need to take.

And He told them this parable, saying, "What man among you, if he has a hundred sheep and has lost one of them, does not leave the ninety-nine in the open pasture, and go after the one which is lost, until he finds it? And when he has found it, he lays it on his shoulders, rejoicing. And when he comes home, he calls together his friends and his neighbors, saying to them, 'Rejoice with me, for I have found my sheep which was lost!' I tell you that in the same way, there will be more joy in heaven over one sinner who repents, than over ninety-nine righteous persons who need no repentance. ... In the same way, I tell you, there will be joy in the presence of the angels of God over one sinner who repents." (Luke 15:3–7; 10)

Observe how the lilies of the field grow; they do not toil nor do they spin, yet I say to you that even Solomon in all his glory did not clothe himself like one of these. But if God so arrays the grass of the field, which is alive today and tomorrow is thrown into the furnace, will He not much more do for you, O men of little faith? ... But seek first His kingdom and His righteousness; and all these things shall be added to you. Therefore do not be anxious for tomorrow; for tomorrow will care for itself. Each day has enough trouble of its own. (Matthew 6:28–30; 33–34)

Christ continually teaches us not to be upset or anxious in any circumstance. We need to learn how to live in the moment. So why do we have the genetic inclination to worry about everything? I had to smile with God one day and chuckle at myself during a major rainstorm. During this storm, we received about one inch of rain in less than one hour. A very wide-eyed and drenched baby squirrel took shelter and huddled as tightly as it could on the tray of my bird feeder, under the "roof" that protected the birdseed. It just barely fit! The finches were taking shelter on the drain pipe, under the overhang of the house. When the rain stopped, they all talked up a storm. The sound was loud and beautiful as they praised the Lord for His perfect provision during the storm. Their Creator God did His part to provide for their needs; all they had to do was be patient, wait, and rest in His provision ... and then give Him all the praise and glory!

Soon after, I came across this anonymous quote, which I found to be powerful: "Faith looks across the storm—it doesn't doubt or stop to look at the clouds and things without. Faith doesn't question why when all His ways are hard to understand, but trusts and prays." Jonah saw God do a remarkable thing in the lives of the people who lived in Nineveh. And if Jonah was filled with discouragement and selfishness, hopefully he overcame it and rejoiced in God's amazing grace and restoration.

Keeping your focus and direction are important regardless of the circumstance, environment, or the outcome of what surrounds you in your life journey. If you live (or have traveled) in a location that has winter snowstorms, you are familiar with the residue that covers the roadways after a storm from the sand and sprays that the road crews put on the roads to help keep us safe. I have had a couple of instances in my life when I have driven straight down the road only to realize—or in one case be pulled over by the police who informed me that I was erratically driving down the road—weaving from side to side. Not! I was driving straight down the road, and properly on my side of the road. How could that happen? Well, the sand and spray residue had covered the lane markings, and I truly wasn't in my proper lane. There were turn lanes, special markings for narrowing the traffic flow, and so on, and I wasn't driving the road as the city planner had determined was appropriate for that particular street. What appeared to be a straight road was truly a road that weaved from side to side. This caused me to reflect on God's highway and the road He has called us to walk. In a sense, everyone's path is headed in the same direction. But has the "world" changed the course, so we end up weaving to and fro as we travel this road of life? One road weaves and leads to destruction, and the Lord's road leads to eternal life. Oh to recognize the correct markings on the journey road of life and follow His directions. And as with any roadway, there are stop signs, stoplights, and other traffic signs to guide you safely on your way. So it is with God's Word, the Bible. His Word will guide you and provide encouragement and instruction for your life journey. Allow your Heavenly Father to use His Word to define who you are.

Choose to be led by the strong hand of God, not the half-truths of the voices of the world that seek to destroy and define you by wearing you out and causing you regrets. What voices have you chosen to listen to? Are they voices of misguided intentions and expectations? Wrap yourself in His mercy, grace, and strength, like an extra-large winter coat on an extremely cold winter day. Let Him hold and protect you! You are a child of the Majestic God and redeemed by the blood of His Son, Jesus Christ. Discover God's extravagant love under, in, and through any circumstance. Don't be a Jonah, who chooses to be self-centered in his misinterpretation of a successful circumstance.

Trusting and believing in God's abundant and detailed care for you is life changing and happens one day at a time. Sometimes it is one second at a time. One of the first lessons to learn is that of trust. Trusting Jesus in your life journey and obeying His leading is important. Letting Him take control, guide and lead you, resting in His arms when you have no more to give, and rejoicing and praising Him for His provision at any juncture of your journey brings fulfillment, peace, and joy to your life.

Rejoice always; pray without ceasing; in everything give thanks; for this is God's will for you in Christ Jesus. (1 Thessalonians 5:16–18)

The magnificence and power of God are often revealed to us through nature. The northern lights were spectacular while we were in Churchill. One gentleman on our tour mentioned they made him feel like he was inside God's snow globe, and God was drawing pictures just for him on the outside of the globe to enjoy. The northern lights painted a heavenly display of God's power and creativity. Every day God has daily blessings prepared for you to enjoy. Watch for them! Your Father God is acting on your behalf, not against you in this earthly journey called life.

Jonah, however, lost sight of God's vision, purpose, and blessings. He lost a thankful and grateful heart, which allowed him to become defined by his weary, tired, and regretful feelings from the circumstance and surroundings in which he found himself. Do you think Jonah allowed regret to take over due to his interpretation of the circumstance, which could end up impacting his character? What do you base your decision on? How do you or your friends allow regret and grief to define your life? Why is this not a wise choice? God is your healer and your shepherd. His provision for you is a constant gift each day. The daily blessings He provides for you are often taken for granted or ignored. A TV station covering an Oklahoma tornado one summer interviewed a man who demonstrated an amazing attitude. The TV video revealed a man who came out of his storm shelter to find everything he and his family owned completely gone responding, "The Lord gave and the Lord has taken away. Blessed be the name of the Lord" (Job 1:21b). Despite his life circumstance and loss, he hadn't lost sight of who God is and how God works on his behalf each day. He still had his life, his family, and they were safe.

We don't hear much about Jonah after his journey to Nineveh. I often wonder if Jonah humbled his heart before God, asked for God's help, and no longer allowed weariness and unhappiness to define his life. Or did he become a bitter, angry, and sorrowful man for the remainder of his life because he chose not to move beyond his self-seeking choices?

Are you or is someone you know similar to Jonah? Are you defined by regret resulting from feeling worn and tired? What causes these regrets to take up residence in your life? Are these qualities motivated by being self-absorbed or selfishness, failing to act on a gift of kindness or an appropriate word, not knowing if the opportunity will ever present itself again or be resolved? Maybe your regrets and unhappiness come from the loss of a job, loss of a loved one, or not being able to take back unkind words. Possibly your unhappiness and regrets are the results of making bad choices, or the lack of taking action in a certain circumstance. Do you run from life's circumstances (good or bad), or do you sit and pout because the outcome isn't what you wanted it to be? The saying that it takes less energy and fewer muscles to smile than it does to frown is true. It takes a lot less energy to be happy and joyful than it does to be worn, tired, and filled with regret. Lord Jesus, help me want to seek You and find You in the painful, broken, and dark places of my life.

You never know when those defining or refining moments may come into your life journey. How do your choices and actions shape your attitudes, character, and future? Review Jonah's choices and their impact on the lives of others and his own life. How was God's testimony and purposes impacted by Jonah's actions? How can you apply these lessons to your own life? How can you apply what you have learned from Jonah's life journey to help a friend who is defined by discouragement and disappointment and help him or her move toward purpose and restored joy?

If I shut up the heavens so that there is no rain, or if I command the locust to devour the land, or if I send pestilence among My people, and My people who are called by My name humble themselves and pray, and seek My face and turn from their wicked ways, then I will hear from heaven, will forgive their sin, and will heal their land. (2 Chronicles 7:13–14)

Don't carry or harbor resentment. Share your faith, walk the walk, talk the talk and shake the dust of judgmental and hurtful feelings. Rest in the Lord's strong and powerful hand, and allow Him to take care of the results of the broken pieces that make you weary, fatigued, and defined by regret. Choose to live for Him and be defined by His purpose and restored joy! Pursue contentment and encouragement, so you may know the sweetness of Christ's joy in any circumstance.

For Further Thought

What circumstance/environment do you see in Jonah's life that challenged his walk with God? How did he handle this circumstance/environment in his life?

What resources did Jonah rely on?

How did God/Jesus Christ act on his behalf?

What can you learn from Jonah's life journey?

How did this circumstance/environment define Jonah's character?

How can you apply these lessons to your life or for a friend?

My study of Jonah prompts me to trust God for _____, _____, and _____. I will _____ in order to trust God more completely with this circumstance/environment in my life.

A Lesson from a Polar Bear
Discernment—Psalms 100:3
Speak When Necessary

The polar bear does not live in isolation. He interacts not only with his own species, but with other species on a daily basis. His daily circumstances and environment may result in altercations or a need to discern what has crossed his path. Through Jonah's journey he also learned the importance of honest communication with God and others. May you be quiet and know the Most Holy God. May you hear the power of His voice and know that He will speak and talk with you whatever the moment, whatever the concern, whatever the day brings your way. May God bring friends alongside you who know when to speak and when to be silent as you journey together. Know that you don't always have to have something to say in response. May the power of the Risen Christ enfold you daily and give you strength, grace, and peace with each new day!

4 Shaking the Dust of Pride, Resentment and Deceit - Defined by Honesty, Integrity, and Selflessness

Many voices speak to you each day. However, there are certain events, circumstances, a song, a friend, a thought, an illness, and so on that stop you in your tracks. Are these voices valid or misguided expectations based on worldly standards? Are they telling you the truth, or are they deceiving you? How you respond to the voices significantly impacts the outcome of your life. The choices you make show what voices you allow to guide your life values and principles. The values and principles you follow are what make up your character. These character qualities are built on a moment-by-moment basis throughout the course of your lifetime. What impacts you at the core of your being? What establishes your integrity of character? What strengthens the moral fiber of your life? What makes you stand up for honesty, compassion, and respect in your sphere of influence? Is it the voice of the Lord, speaking and guiding you on your journey, or a voice that seeks to destroy and beat you up? As a child of God, you need to listen to what He tells you. Do not listen to the world and the lies it tries to impress on you as being truths. Listen to God and seek the lordship of His mercy and grace. Wrap yourself up in Him; let Jesus hold and protect you. You are a child of the Redeeming God. He has rescued you, and you are secure in the Lord Jesus Christ forever!

During the winter months, I love to go for walks in the snow. The quietness and purity of the crystalline falling snow soothes the chaos of my day-to-day life. Before heading outdoors, I need to wrap myself up in winter attire to be safe and protected in order to face the harsh elements outside, darkness, wet snow, slippery footing, and the possibility of wind chill.

This was true of our time in Churchill. One could tell by our wardrobe that our tour group wasn't used to the extreme, wintery temperatures: heavy stocking caps, hooded air force parkas, mitten liners and mittens, sock liners and socks, sturdy boots (tucked with heat inserts to protect our toes from the bitter cold), long underwear, warm shirts, sweaters, windbreakers, and so on. Our layering kept us safe and protected against any circumstance or environment that would present itself during the day's outing. Each of us had put time, thought, and energy into making sure we remained warm in the harsh environment we encountered during our time in Churchill.

There are many similarities between wrapping up and putting on the proper attire for heading out into the cold and darkness of a wintery night and wrapping up in Jesus Christ for your life journey with Him. In Ephesians 6 you are reminded to put on the full armor of God. By wrapping yourself up in Christ, you will be safe and protected against the circumstances and surroundings that may catch you off guard. By allowing God's Holy Spirit to be in control, He will guide you. You will be able to discern His path and be able to move forward, trusting and obeying what He has instructed you to "put on" as His precious child (Colossians 3:8–17).

Your head needs to be protected by the helmet of salvation. Many obstacles in your world will seek to distract your eyes and set your mind against the things of Christ. This "warm hat" helps to keep you focused on the path and enables you to concentrate on God's promises of His love and redemptive salvation in Jesus Christ. Memorizing special Scripture verses to recall at a time of doubt or uncertainty are important protective attire. This enables you to scatter the arrows that the world sends in your direction and reminds you that you are secure in Him.

The breastplate of righteousness covers the torso of your body. Without your heavy winter coat in extremely cold temperatures, it would be very difficult to stay outside for very long. By wrapping up and protecting your heart in God's Word through prayer, Bible study, coming alongside a group of committed friends, and by diligently protecting the Lord's rightful place in your life, your priorities will reveal the evidence of purity, humility, and a genuine love for those around you.

You are to gird your loins (legs) with the truth. Your legs propel you as you walk from destination to destination throughout the day. Fill your day with prayer and listening to the Lord; read or listen to Scripture tapes, listen to Christian music, exercise your muscle of faith (Hebrews 11) as you move through the day's rough circumstances and events, compose a prayer journal to put your prayer requests in writing, record the evidence of God's faithfulness in your life, ask others to stand in the gap and pray for you, and so on.

The shield of faith and the sword of the Spirit of God are important for your offense against the battles you face each day. By trusting and obeying the Lord, you will be defined by Him as a child of the King of Kings! Daily shod your feet with the gospel of peace as you go out into the harsh elements of your world. By knowing why you believe in Jesus Christ you can tell those you meet each day what your relationship with Him means to you and what He has done in your life. Through sharing the gospel of Jesus Christ, you share the gifts of hope, love, peace, confidence, joy, kindness, and self-control. Take the gospel of peace to work, to school, to the grocery store, help serve a meal at the homeless shelter, visit an assisted living facility, or volunteer at church or with a nonprofit that matches your life's passions. Connect with those around you, and allow God to use you in their lives. By giving of yourself to others, your faith becomes real.

How is your life defined? Do you carry baggage with you that hides the real you? Often when you attend a social gathering, you are asked to wear a name tag. Depending on the type of event, you may be asked to tell a little about yourself. Too often we judge our worth by our last name, our job or position within a company, how much we make, what part of town we live in, where our children attend school, what level of education we completed, what church we attend, who your spouse is or isn't … you get the idea. At an event you may also be asked, "Well then you would know Sam. Boy is he bitter and angry. How do you work with him?" If you are like me, you don't want to be known or defined by bad attitudes or a downtrodden outlook on life. How do your actions and choices reveal who you are in this life journey? What does your name say about you? When individuals hear your name, do they think about your positive character or an overwhelming negative attitude that defines your life's choices?

… choose for yourselves today whom you will serve: … but as for me and my house, we will serve the Lord. (Joshua 24:15)

The exciting thing about being a follower of Jesus Christ is that you are defined by His forgiveness and love, by His mercy and grace, by His peace and joy. You are defined by the shed blood of Jesus Christ, and you are secure in Him. You are forgiven in Jesus Christ and have been reborn as a child of God! You are a new creation in Christ. You are redefined by His love, mercy, and grace! When the going gets tough and you need to choose to seek His help, even if your only prayer is, "Lord, help me," that is okay. Or you may say, "Thank you, Jesus, for standing in the midst of my darkness and holding me safe and secure in your care and provision. Help me to make choices that cause my life to follow you. Thank you for the power of the Holy Spirit to see this come about in my life regardless of how steep the mountainside or how deep the valley may become. I choose this day to follow You and You alone."

It is at this point in your life journey that you can watch God's provision and transforming power at work in you! Your days were numbered before you were born. You are very special in God's sight. Your Father has a perfect plan for you. Move forward in confidence and obedience, and rest in His faithful provision, love, and care daily. He has your best interests at heart.

Negative and downtrodden attitudes are life perspectives that are extremely draining. They will zap you of your energy, dreams, life, joy, and peace. Basically, they will eat you alive! Don't be a complainer about the darkness. Instead, be a candle of light in the darkness and shine for Jesus. Look for the good in everything that comes your way. Give thanks for the blessings you have been given, as the negative times will not last forever. Through the pain and difficult moments of life, seek to learn the lessons of compassion, mercy, forgiveness, love, grace, patience, endurance, and contentment, and become a brilliant and pure light for the Lord Jesus. Move beyond your limitations, and focus on the hidden blessings God has provided. Stand strong as a child of the Lord God Almighty. Rise to the occasion set before you because of the strength only He can instill within you through His Holy Spirit as you reach out beyond yourself to others.

Joseph's Journey

Joseph is an incredible example for us on how to shake off the dust and rise above unfair circumstances and a less than favorable environment. Throughout his life, Joseph repeatedly rose above unjust circumstances to be a man of true integrity, honesty, and resilient character. His life shows us how wrong intentions made right by God's all-knowing protection, His direct action, and perfect timing (on Joseph's behalf and for future generations) resulted in God turning a misguided family decision into something very positive and lifesaving. God's purposes will, at all times, work everything together for good. Sometimes you will see these results, and at other times, you will just need to trust God and take Him at His Word. In your sorrow and pain, worship Him for His sovereign care and provision for your current circumstances and future. Your life may not look like how you would picture it, but God is still present and walking with—or carrying—you every step of the way.

Genesis Chapter 37:1–11

You will see in Genesis 37 that Joseph's father's had a strong love and affection for him. As a result, Joseph held a favored spot in his father's eyes. Joseph's brothers hated and resented the fact Joseph held this position of high esteem. Their hatred was so strong toward Joseph that even their conversations with him weren't friendly (Genesis 37:4). In Genesis 37:5–11, Joseph tells his brothers about two dreams he had. As a result his brothers became even more infuriated with him. They didn't like any dream that indicated Joseph would someday reign over them. He was their boastful kid brother. Who did he think he was anyway?

Genesis Chapter 37:12–36

The brothers' jealousy, bitterness, and resentment continued to grow. Eventually they took advantage of an opportunity to plot harm against their brother. Joseph's father had sent him to find his brothers, who were pasturing the family flocks, to obtain news of how they were doing. When they saw Joseph coming, they plotted to take his life. Rueben, the oldest of Joseph's brothers, was able to modify their drastic intentions, and instead, the brothers threw Joseph into a pit. (Rueben's hope and prayer was that he could return at a later time to rescue Joseph from the pit and return him to his father.) Meanwhile, the brothers, enjoying their meal, noticed a caravan approaching. As their conversation unfolded, they questioned if it would profit them to kill their brother, and they determined it would be far better to sell Joseph to the caravan when it passed by. So the brothers sold Joseph to the slave caravan, and he headed to Egypt against his will.

Joseph was in a very desperate situation. As he sat in the pit, he most likely knew his life was on the line. Was he excited to be sold into slavery and headed off to Egypt? Did he go quietly? Was he anxious about what would unfold in the days ahead? How would these slave traders treat him? He was probably unsure of where this new "adventure" would take him, but Joseph was still alive and had options awaiting him as each new day unfolded. Joseph knew his God was with him and would provide for his needs. There are times in your life—or in the life of a loved one—that you may also feel trapped in a pit, cornered and unsure of what the future will hold. As you trust the Holy Spirit one moment at a time, God will help and show you how to rebuild your life in the days, weeks, months, and years ahead. Learning to pray, trust, and rest in Almighty God's hand of grace and mercy is an important decision for you to build into your life's responses.

Genesis Chapter 39:1–23

After his arrival in Egypt, Joseph was sold to the captain of Pharaoh's bodyguard, Potiphar. Potiphar was observant and noticed everything Joseph did prospered, because the Lord was with him (Genesis 39:2–6). As a result, Potiphar made Joseph master over his entire household and everything he owned.

Joseph was handsome in appearance, and Potiphar's wife noticed. Day after day, Joseph refused her sinful advances. Until one day, Potiphar's wife lied and said Joseph tried to rape her. Immediately, Potiphar threw Joseph into prison, and again Joseph found himself penalized for taking a stand for honesty, morality, and integrity, and for behaving as he should in a difficult circumstance and environment (Genesis 39:11–20).

But the Lord was with Joseph and extended kindness to him, and gave him favor in the sight of the chief jailer. (Genesis 39:21)

Once in prison, the jailer also noted the Lord God was with Joseph, and he, too, placed everything under Joseph's supervision. Joseph's words and actions spoke loudly. To have someone notice his countenance and character by how his life was defined and lived (not by his circumstances and surroundings) through his faith and trust in the Lord God Almighty speaks volumes. Joseph knew he was a child of the King and that his Mighty God would walk with him and provide, regardless of where his life journey took him moment by moment each day.

"I Love Thee, O Lord, my strength." The Lord is my rock and my fortress and my deliverer; My God, my rock, in whom I take refuge; My shield and the horn of my salvation, my stronghold. I call upon the Lord, who is worthy to be praised, And I am saved from my enemies … But the Lord was my

stay. He brought me forth also into a broad place; He rescued me, because He delighted in me. (Psalm 18:1–3; 18–19)

Genesis Chapter 40:1–23

In chapter 40 you find two of Pharaoh's staff—the cupbearer and the baker—thrown into prison for questionable actions they had taken. Both had unique dreams, and naturally, they were perplexed and upset about the dreams. They were eager to find someone who would be able to discern what these dreams meant (Genesis 40:8). The Lord God Almighty had revealed to Joseph the interpretation of their dreams. Joseph eagerly explained the meaning of the dreams to both the cupbearer and the baker. Within three days, the cupbearer was restored to his position, but the baker, unfortunately, was executed. The cupbearer promised Joseph he would remember him to Pharaoh but quickly forgot all about him (Genesis 40:20–23).

What is it that really makes your life valuable? Is it places, things, people, money, success, or what? What do you think Joseph valued the most in his life and why? Joseph's life was noticed by all who came in contact with him. At some point one would have to wonder if Joseph questioned how much bad luck he was going to be inflicted with on his life journey. He was tossed into a pit, sold into slavery, thrown into prison unjustly, and then forgotten by the cupbearer, who may have seemed like his only hope for restitution and release. But Joseph wasn't defined by his circumstances and environment. He knew God was ever present with him, guiding and blessing his every thought, word, and action. Joseph was optimistic and knew from the past that God would provide and remain faithful in the present and future regardless of the string of bad luck he continued to encounter on his life journey. He was quick to forgive. Joseph knew how to live above his surroundings, lived a purpose-filled life, and was fulfilled right where God had planted him. He chose to have a positive attitude despite the ways his surroundings impacted his life. As a result, Joseph's sphere of influence and the people around him were changed regardless of the circumstance and environment he found himself.

Who or what is your enemy? When I hear the word "enemy," I usually think of countries at odds with my homeland. What if you were to view the word "enemy" as those things that cause you to define yourself inaccurately? What if the enemy is an activity, an attitude, something that provides you with the opportunity to make a poor choice that will define you in either a manner that is not appropriate or an accurate portrayal of your character? How does the Almighty God see you as you move through this circumstance(s)? Will He see you as He saw Joseph—honest, full of integrity, and moral in your decisions and actions?

Joseph had plenty of opportunities to define his character by his experiences such as discouragement, resentment, and deception. These character attributes had been modeled for him at home for seventeen years, before his brothers sold him into slavery and sent him packing to Egypt. Joseph also had opportunities to be bitter, disappointed, and full of regrets for what might have been had these circumstances not taken place. But Joseph chose not to walk that walk. Did Joseph have rough days and discouraging thoughts? Did he shed tears of sorrow? I am sure he did, but Joseph chose to not allow those attitudes to control and define his life journey. Joseph lived his life intentionally and moved toward his Everlasting Father's care for every circumstance and environment that surrounded his life journey. He placed his faith, trust, hope, and confidence in his Majestic God.

Let me hear Thy lovingkindness in the morning; for I trust in Thee; Teach me the way in which I should walk; For to Thee I lift up my soul. Deliver me, O Lord, from my enemies; I take refuge in Thee. Teach me to do Thy will, For Thou art my God; Let Thy good spirit lead me on level ground. For the sake of Thy name, O Lord, revive me. In Thy lovingkindness bring my soul out of trouble. (Psalm 143:8–11)

Joseph must have been an expert at casting his burdens upon the Lord and not taking them back. Like Joseph, you need to give everything up to God and leave it at His feet. Your Father God will sustain you. He will not allow you to be shaken, and He will deliver you. What you place at the feet of the Lord in prayer leave at the throne of grace and mercy. Stay focused on His provisions, and don't take back your burdens, even for a moment. Easier said than done, but remember God knows what you are made of—flesh and blood. Talk to your Father about the good, the bad, and the ugly. Talk to Him over and over (and over again) if you need to. It is okay! He already knows your thought before you think it, and He does love you. With the help of His Holy Spirit, you will be able to move above the circumstance and trust Jesus Christ for your deliverance. Like Joseph you may find that your deliverance may only be in your heart and attitude. God may allow you to stay amid the circumstance, or He may move you out of the darkness of the canyon you find yourself trudging through. Joseph had learned how to rest in the powerful and mighty hands of God as a youth, and as a young adult, continued to trust God with his life. From the mountaintop or darkest canyon of your life journey, are you willing to trust God? Are you willing to trust Him with the circumstances and/or surroundings of your life when they don't make any sense to you?

He will redeem my soul in peace from the battle which is against me, For they are many who strive with me. God will hear and answer them - ... Cast your burden on the Lord, and He will sustain you; He will never allow the righteous to be shaken. (Psalm 55:18–19, 22)

Blessed be the Lord, who daily bears our burden, The God who is our salvation. God is to us a God of deliverances; And to God the Lord belongs the escapes of death. (Psalm 68:19–20)

Genesis Chapter 41:1–57

After two years passed, the cupbearer heard Pharaoh needed someone to interpret his dream. It was at this time that the cupbearer remembered Joseph. The cupbearer told Pharaoh he met a young man in prison who had accurately interpreted his dream. As a result, Pharaoh sent for Joseph and told him his dream (Genesis 41:14–36). God revealed the interpretation to

Joseph. In Joseph's opening comments to Pharaoh about his dream, Joseph acknowledged the Lord God Almighty by stating, "God has shown to Pharaoh what He is about to do" (Genesis 41:28). Joseph explained to Pharaoh there would be seven years of plenty followed by seven years of drought and famine. Believing God's Word, Pharaoh exonerated Joseph and placed him in charge of his household. Only by the throne was Pharaoh greater than Joseph, as Joseph was set over all of the land of Egypt (Genesis 41:39–45). In Joseph's late thirties, his life changed quickly and dramatically. In the years to come, God's plan for seven years of plenty followed by seven years of severe drought and famine unfolded just as Joseph had foretold. But again, Joseph's circumstance and environment didn't impact the choices he made or how his life was defined. He wasn't defined by pride or arrogance but set forth to bring about a positive change for everyone in the land as God's perfect plan began to unfold. And remember God's perfect plan began with Joseph being sold into slavery … and he, too, experienced the seven years of plenty and the seven years of famine.

Genesis Chapters 42–46:7

Chapter 42:1–5 provides you with an ongoing account of the dysfunctional family dynamic that had continued over time with Joseph's family back in Israel. In verses 1 and 2, Jacob (the father of the family) gets the attention of his adult children by stating, "Why are you staring at one another? … Behold I have heard that there is grain in Egypt; go down there and buy some for us from that place, so that we may live and not die." Also in verse 4, we see that Jacob didn't send his youngest son, as he was afraid harm might befall Benjamin on the journey. Some things never change.

Chapter 42:6 confirms that Joseph remained the ruler over the land and was the one who sold grain to all the people of the land. When Joseph's brothers arrived, they bowed down before their brother, with their faces to the ground. Joseph recognized them, but he disguised himself so they didn't recognize him. It was then that Joseph remembered the dream he had about them when he was seventeen years old and they sold him into slavery. Chapters 42 through 45 give the account of Joseph's brothers going back and forth between Israel and Egypt to buy grain and their interactions with Joseph. Eventually, Jacob and Benjamin came with the brothers to relocate and live in Egypt.

Take time to read the entire account of their interactions and God's provision for Joseph's family. In Chapter 45:1–7, Joseph reveals himself to his brothers and affirms God sent him before them to preserve life. The account provides a heartfelt glimpse of the intense emotions felt on both sides, Reuben's ongoing love for Joseph and the recognition of the wrong done to him years prior were evident, as was the anxiety of the brothers once they knew the Egyptian leader was their brother. Joseph wept at their bittersweet reunion. What the brothers had meant for harm, God, looking ahead, had meant for good. Joseph's life exemplifies God's perfect plan and timing. God's extravagant ministry of love, mercy, and grace for all His children can be seen through His extended favor as He works on behalf of His children to protect and draw them closer to His side.

Throughout Joseph's life, he had ample opportunities to allow his character to be impacted by his circumstances and the environment that surrounded him. How would you respond to the circumstances Joseph found himself in? Would you have felt like shaking your fist at God and saying, "Really?" Joseph, however, chose to trust God with the outcome of whatever situation he found himself. As you look back on Joseph's life—sold as a slave, put in prison, forgotten, and then restored to a position of respect and honor—one can see the life lessons he learned along his journey prepared him for his (God's) future. Joseph's life journey demonstrates for you the importance of making wise and godly choices that will not allow you to become bitter, discouraged, discontented, resentful, full of regrets, grudges, and so on. Joseph could have easily (and in some ways justifiably so) become a man who looked at his circumstances and surroundings and chosen a negative and completely different outcome for his life and for those in his sphere of influence. Joseph was defined by his faith and trust in the Lord God Almighty! For Joseph, God was enough. Is He enough for you? Do you trust the King of Kings with your life journey and how it is defined? How do you handle shattered expectations? Dear Father God, give me the strength and wisdom to trust and rest in You and remain hidden in the secure palm of Your protective hand.

Remember to pray at all times, regardless of the level of pain or frustration, as you walk through the storm, wind, rain, and fire of the circumstances of your journey. Bury the pain and *fill in the blank*, and leave it at the throne of grace and mercy at the feet of Jesus Christ. Leave it behind; don't go looking for the what-ifs" ... well, if this would have happened, or why did this happen now, why are they doing this, how could they? Had Joseph allowed these types of torturous thoughts to follow and define him as he headed off to Egypt, the days ahead of him would have been needlessly painful and unpleasant.

Be anxious for nothing, but in everything by prayer and supplication with thanksgiving let your requests be made known to God. And the peace of God, which surpasses all comprehension, shall guard your hearts and your mind in Christ Jesus. Finally, brethren, whatever is true, whatever is honorable, whatever is right, whatever is pure, whatever is lovely, whatever is of good repute, if there is any excellence and anything worthy of praise, let your mind dwell on these things. (Philippians 4:6–8)

Since then we have a great high priest who has passed through the heavens, Jesus, the Son of God, let us hold fast our confession. For we do not have a high priest who cannot sympathize with our weaknesses, but one who has been tempted in all things as we are, yet without sin. Let us therefore draw near with confidence to the throne of grace, that we may receive mercy and may find grace to help in time of need. (Hebrews 4:14–16)

Your Father God is transforming you into a new person daily. Leave your darkness, and move into the light of Jesus Christ's love and forgiveness. Ask God to show you how to make the right choices—the best choices—knowing you can trust God and that He has your best interests close to His heart. You have been set free in Jesus Christ. God's love is extravagant. It led His Son to the cross to die and be resurrected from the grave in order to restore you into a right relationship with Him. Choose not to live in the past. Move toward the light, and let the cold and icy dust fall away in the warmth of His eternal love. Be defined in Christ ... and by Him alone.

As a Christian, your life journey will not be an easy one. Life will never be perfect, no matter how you envision it. But Christ has promised to walk with you and guide you as you trust Him moment by moment with the circumstances and environments that life brings your way. Your life on earth is an adventure, and you must approach it with hope and faith that God always has your best interests at heart. Do not allow the bumps in the road to rob you of your joy in Jesus Christ!

The Son of God, Jesus Christ, wasn't treated fairly during His life journey here on earth either. He understands where you are and what you are going through. He has immense love, mercy, and grace to carry you through the storms, wind, rain, and fire of your life journey. No circumstance that concerns you will catch Him off guard. "Jesus Christ is the same yesterday and today, yes and forever" (Hebrews 13:8). He has already walked with (or carried) you through the storm, wind, rain, and fire. He will hold you firmly in His hand and see you through to the other side! Seek His face continually in prayer and trust Him.

How are you defined?

I am sure there were times when Joseph felt like a square peg in a round hole. Have you ever felt like that—out of place and not sure what to do? It isn't a bad thing to be the square peg. As you take your walk with Jesus seriously, you may feel like a square peg in a round hole. There have been times in my life when I have felt like that square peg, and it hurt not to fit into the hole everyone else was trying to fit in. Often when I have felt this way it was because the world was trying to make me fit its mold. Your God is holy, and He has set you apart as His child; you aren't of this world. The thinking and actions of the world are foreign to what you are called to be and live as you walk your journey based on your Christian faith. When you feel this way, question what it is that makes you react this way. What are your life choices telling you about yourself and what you esteem to be important? What is the pressure you are feeling trying to tell you? Are you off base in your thinking? Are you being insensitive and self-centered? Are you trying to be something you aren't, or are you involved in something you shouldn't be involved in? Listen, pray, and trust God. He will lead and confirm what is in your heart.

> *... greater is He who is in you than he who is in the world. (1 John 4:4)*

By observing Joseph's brothers, one can see that following after pride, resentment, and deceit in one's life choices can enslave and rob you of happiness, peace, and purpose in life. Honesty with yourself liberates. Pursue honesty in all areas of your life as you focus on integrity and selflessness. God may choose to use lessons about honesty in your life to teach you more about His great love and care for you. Rest in His perfect plan, and know He is there, orchestrating His perfect plan for your life journey.

Over the years I have often heard Christian teachers refer to an illustration of how God views our life as a beautiful and exquisite tapestry. Our Everlasting Father views the tapestry as complete and sees the beautiful weavings, colors, textures, and the entire image displayed in all its final grandeur from the front side of the tapestry. Most of the time we are limited in our view and only see our tapestry from the backside and usually choose to view one small section at a time. It you have ever looked at the back of a tapestry, it really is billions of threads intertwined together. To be honest, from the backside, the weaving really looks more like a mess than something of beauty. When turned to the right side, it becomes a marvelous image for all to enjoy. So it is in your life journey, when you only see the tapestry from the backside and only choose to see small sections of tangled and often messy thread work. Have you ever felt like you were getting tangled up in the threads? Have you found it hard to get out of the tangled mess? I have! Nevertheless, your Father, the Creator of the universe, always sees immense beauty in you! He always holds you in the palm of His hand, and He will forever hold you increasingly close to His heart! You are a child of God—the God of all ages, the King of Kings, and Lord of Lords. He cares intimately about you, your feelings, your happiness, and your future. You must rest in His provision and craftsmanship to make your tapestry become the elegant weaving He intended it to be. Joseph knew how to surrender and allow God to weave His beauty into his life despite the tangled messes he found himself in. God is good; He can be no other!

For Further Thought

What circumstance/environment do you see in Joseph's life that challenged his walk with God? How did he handle this circumstance/environment?

What resources did Joseph rely on?

How did God/Jesus Christ act on his behalf?

What lessons can you learn from Joseph's life journey?

How did this circumstance/environment define Joseph's character?

How can you apply these lessons to your life or for a friend's?

My study of Joseph prompts me to trust God for _____, _____, and _____. I will _____ in order to trust God more completely with this circumstance/environment in my life.

Ruth's Journey

> *Though I walk in the midst of trouble, Thou wilt revive me; Thou will stretch forth Thy hand against the wrath of my enemies, And Thy hand will save me. The Lord will accomplish what concerns me; Thy lovingkindness, O Lord, is everlasting; Do not forsake the works of Thy hands. (Psalm 138:7–8)*

Throughout Ruth's relationship with her mother-in-law, Naomi, you see a woman who demonstrates love, loyalty, dedication, and trust. Although Ruth's life journey included joy and deep sorrow, her loyalty to Naomi resulted in triumph and blessing due to her honesty, integrity, and selflessness.

> *The Lord lives, and blessed be my rock; And exalted be the God of my salvation. (Psalm 18:46)*

Ruth Chapter 1

In chapter 1, you learn Naomi's husband and sons have died, leaving her and her two daughters-in-law widowed. Due to these circumstances, Naomi decided she would leave Moab and return to the city of Bethlehem, in Israel, her homeland. She encourages her two daughters-in-law to remain in Moab with their families and begin a new life with her blessing. Orpah chooses to remain in Moab. However, Ruth refused to leave Naomi and wanted to go to Bethlehem with her to begin a new life. Ruth's outlook on the future was optimistic, and she welcomed a new adventure—a new normal—with Naomi as they walked together with their Heavenly Father, their Redeemer and provider, the Most Holy God of the ages. Because Naomi could see Ruth's determination and love to follow and go with her, they departed together for Israel. They arrived at harvest time.

> *But Ruth said, "Do not urge me to leave you or turn back from following you; for where you go, I will go, and*

where you lodge, I will lodge. Your people shall be my
people, and your God will be my God. (Ruth 1:16)

Ruth Chapter 2

Chapter 2 finds Ruth leaving early in the morning to go and glean grain for Naomi and herself in order for them to be able to prepare a meal and eat. Ruth finds a field, asks permission to glean behind the reapers, and spends the day diligently harvesting the grain that fell by the wayside in the fields. The field belongs to Boaz, who just happens to be a wealthy kinsman of Naomi's. Boaz inquires about Ruth and is impressed with the report of her commitment to Naomi and to God. "May the Lord reward your work, and your wages be full from the Lord, the God of Israel, under whose wings you have come to seek refuge." (Ruth 2:12)

Boaz makes sure Ruth knows she is welcome in his field and that she should only come to his fields to glean behind his reapers. Ruth bows to Boaz in humility, thanking him for his hospitality and grace. Out of compassion, Boaz instructs his reapers to leave extra grain behind for Ruth to harvest. On arriving home and preparing a meal for Naomi and herself, Naomi recognizes that God's favor has been resting on Ruth. After inquiring about whose field she had been gleaning in, Naomi tells Ruth that Boaz is a very close family relative.

Your expectations and dreams throughout your life journey must be held with open hands. God will take out and place blessings into your hands as He sees best. Some, but not all, of your personal expectations will be met. Ruth knew the All-Knowing God would do His part to provide for all their needs, regardless of what circumstances or surroundings they might encounter. She knew God would go with them, take them safely on their life journey together, and protect them all the way. Knowing the Almighty God was active in Naomi's life, and recognizing this same God was also her true and faithful God, was something that defined Ruth's character. The Almighty Sovereign God was her rock and her strength. She knew He was always faithful and would carry her, regardless of what unfolded in her future. Did she wonder how things would turn out? Did she encounter fears and concerns? Probably yes. Did she become overly preoccupied and fearful to the point of not being able to take a step forward? I think not.

Sometimes it may be hard for you to remember you are human. You will not be perfect in this lifetime, and you will not be able to make perfect sense out of every rough circumstance and environment that presents itself during your life. Like Ruth, you will continue to live and learn on a daily basis to delight and walk with God as you allow Him to take up His rightful residence in your life. As you have seen, you will need to keep your focus on Jesus Christ. Knowing you are safe and that God will accomplish the desires of His heart, His perfect plan for you, helps when the canyon walls begin to close in on you. As you see your relationship with your Everlasting Father strengthen, remember how He has protected in the past, and He will do it again. Amid the storm, it may be easy to forget His past provision, but remember how He acted on your behalf. He is here today, and He holds your future. Praise God for His faithfulness in your life!

Trust in the Lord, and do good; Dwell in the land and cultivate faithfulness. Delight yourself in the Lord; And He will give you the desires of your heart. Commit your way to the Lord, Trust also in Him, and He will do it. (Psalm 37:3–5)

As for God, His way is blameless; The word of the Lord is tried; He is a shield to all who take refuge in Him. For who is God, but the Lord? And who is a rock, except our God, The God who girds me with strength, And makes my way blameless? He makes my feet like hinds feet, And sets me upon my high places. He trains my hands for battle, So that my arms can bend a bow of bronze. Thou hast also given me the shield of Thy salvation, And Thy right hand upholds me; And Thy gentleness makes me great. Thou dost enlarge my steps under me, And my feet have not slipped. (Psalm 18:30–36)

Ruth Chapters 3–4

The account of Ruth's life in the Bible doesn't provide you a lot of additional personal information. Ruth 3:11 reveals that Ruth was a woman of excellence. The Amplified Bible states Ruth was known throughout the city as "a woman of strength—worth, bravery, capability." Despite the integrity and strength of character, Ruth experienced pain and loss in her journey. If you stop and think about something important you have lost, you may have a glimpse into the loss Ruth probably felt inside: the loss of her spouse at an early age, the loss of potential children and a family she had dreamed for since she was young, leaving her parents and sister to go with Naomi to a country she had never seen before, wondering if she would ever see her family again, and so on. Resentment was not a part of her life responses. Ruth also encountered a lot of new normals in her life journey as she walked alongside her mother-in-law, Naomi. Her journey exhibits loyalty, faithfulness, and patience.

Facing new normals means you will approach circumstances and environments you have loved and cherished from a new perspective. Maybe you used to love to go for walks in a park but can no longer do so for some reason. Find a new park, ride a bike, take a friend who is no longer able to walk for a wheelchair ride or a drive through the park. Adapt the activities that were special, and rebuild them in a new, meaningful way. Remember all the while that although circumstances and environments may never be the way you initially expected them to be, your Father will make the new normal become a cherished blessing(s) in your life in the days ahead. For Ruth to build new meaning and purpose into her life required commitment, confidence, and trust as she put one foot in front of the other each new day. God made her new normal a blessing not only for her but also for Naomi and Boaz. Trust, obey, hope, and walk confidently in His plan for your life.

The responsibility of next of kin was an extended obligation that was honored in Ruth's lifetime. (You can read more about the responsibility of kinship in Deuteronomy 25:5–10.) Chapter 3 finds Ruth following Naomi's instructions and her pursuit to see the responsibility of the next of kin fulfilled by Boaz. Boaz, who is man of integrity, knows of a closer relative, so he contacts this individual to determine what he desires to do in this circumstance. After an open discussion at one of the city gates, it is determined the closest kin will abdicate his responsibility. Boaz then makes Ruth his wife. After their marriage, they had a son named Obeb, who became the grandfather of King David. (Ruth 4:7–13)

How do you think Joseph and Ruth were able to turn negative and troublesome circumstances into something positive in their lives? Both Joseph and Ruth knew the importance of keeping their focus on their Redeemer God. When you seek God in prayer and walk closely by His side moment by moment, your walk through the canyon, valley, or on the mountaintops will allow you to know God's peace. As a result God's peace will blanket you through the thick and thin of any darkness or shadows you may experience. Through your prayers and a thankful heart, you will know the reassurance of Jesus Christ's presence in the storm. God will release the dust and ashes of worn brokenness that have come into your life. And He will define your life by honesty, integrity, and selflessness.

And not only this, but we also exult in our tribulations, knowing that tribulation brings about perseverance; and perseverance, proven character; and proven character hope; and hope does not disappoint, because the love of God has been poured out within our hearts through the Holy Spirit who was given to us. (Romans 5:3–5)

How do you respond or react to the circumstances and environments that surround your life? If you look closely at the things that bring pain to your heart, you might be surprised to find that within the pain lies a huge blessing. How did Joseph and Ruth find blessings in the pain they experienced? Look beyond the normal routines and your comfort zone. Find the blessings outside the known routines of your life, and choose to walk in the newness of the circumstances and blessings present within that moment. Our sole purpose in life is to know and love the Lord our God with all our heart, soul, mind, and strength. Jesus Christ will direct you in every life circumstance in order for you to know Him more fully. Had Joseph and Ruth not gone through the fire, wind, and rain of their storms, they wouldn't have seen the face of God. Your Heavenly Father beckons you to draw nearer to Him.

Where does your strength come from—places, things, people, money, success? How do you find your strength in the Lord? When I feel afraid, unsure, and downtrodden, I turn to God in prayer (often through tears). I read/study my Bible, especially the Psalms. The Psalms will remind you of how big your God truly is; He is the Alpha and the Omega—the beginning and the end. He is all-powerful, all-knowing, ever-present, the great healer and protector. And He is your best friend. How big is your God? He made the heavens and the earth. He formed you in your mother's womb and knows you inside and out. He loves you with an everlasting love that has no limits or boundaries. David wrote many of the psalms recorded in your Bible. In reading his poetry and songs, you will discover that he experienced weariness, fear, pain, and suffering. However, he quickly turned to the Lord God in prayer and worship to find his confidence, trust, and strength. Your strength should come from the Lord. Focus on Him. Keep your eyes on Jesus, the author and perfecter of your faith.

Remembering the ways God has acted on your behalf in the past and what He has done for you will give you hope for the future, especially when circumstances seem unclear or times are rough. When you hurt too deeply for words, remember how Jesus has been faithful to you and others before you, and claim His faithfulness and wisdom in your current circumstances. In your darkest moments, He will be your strength. Jesus Christ is worthy of your trust and confidence. Pursue gratitude in the big and small blessings of your life journey, and it will build your capability to remain strong in the Lord when the going gets tough.

The Lord is my light and my salvation; Whom shall I fear? The Lord is the defense of my life; Whom shall I dread? When evildoers came upon me to devour my flesh, My adversaries and my enemies, they stumbled and fell. Though a host encamp against me, My heart will not fear; Though war arise against me, In spite of this I shall be confident. One thing I have asked from the Lord, that I shall seek: That I may dwell in the house of the Lord all the days of my life, To behold the beauty of the Lord, And to meditate in His temple. For in the day of trouble He will conceal me in His tabernacle; In the secret place of His tent He will hide me: He will lift me up on a rock. And now my head will be lifted up above my enemies around me; And I will offer in His tent sacrifices with shouts of joy; I will sing, yes I will sing praises to the Lord. (Psalm 27:1–6)

For Further Thought

What circumstance/environment do you see in Ruth's life that challenged her walk with God? How did she handle this circumstance/environment in her life?

What resources did Ruth rely on?

How did God/Jesus Christ act on her behalf?

What lessons can you learn from Ruth's life journey?

How did this circumstance/environment define Ruth's character?

How can you apply these lessons to your life or for a friend's?

My study of Ruth prompts me to trust God for _____, _____, and _____. I will _____ in order to trust God more completely with this circumstance/environment in my life.

A Lesson from a Polar Bear
Integrity—Proverbs 4:23
Be Majestic

The polar bear, as it migrates in his frigid terrain to the sheet ice and beyond for a dark, blistery winter of hunting for food to sustain it for the next year, isn't anxious about what lies ahead in the vast white expanse of the subarctic. The polar bear stands strong and proud in who it is, how God created it, and in the journey it has been called to live. In grace and faith you can demonstrate this character quality through your words and actions. The Lord continually speaks to you each day. He will encourage and sustain you in ways that you will marvel at daily!

Our Lord Jesus is majestic in His redeeming love, so continue to seek Him, and He will give you the power to stand strong in the unknown expanse of today and tomorrow.

5 Shaking the Dust of Disappointment and Discouragement - Defined by Belief, Contentment, and Hope

Oh that my words were written! Oh that they were inscribed in a book! That with an iron stylus and lead They were engraved in the rock forever! And as for me, I know that my Redeemer lives, And at the last He will take His stand on the earth. Even after my skin is destroyed, Yet from my flesh I shall see God; Whom I myself shall behold, And whom my eyes shall see and not another. My heart faints within me.

—Job 19:23–27

Contentment results from trusting God as your supplier and showing an attitude of gratefulness by accepting all He provides for you. Having a thankful heart is significant in your life journey! Billy Graham (evangelist, b. AD 1918) said that "The root of discouragement is unbelief." By believing and trusting God with the circumstances of your life, your faith and belief in His defining power multiply.

Nehemiah is a great example of a man of faith. With sleeves rolled up in the thick of the battle, he was able to shake off the dust not only for himself but for those around him. He wasn't defined by the negativity around him. Nor did he allow his circumstances to deplete his motivation and hopeful outlook on life. Nehemiah overcame the obstacles tossed at him as he stepped into the rising, stormy waters and fire surrounding him and pursued a new opportunity that had crushed and discouraged his heart.

If you are a living, breathing, and active human being, you have most likely faced a soul-searching need, and it may have crushed every ounce of energy out of you. It doesn't matter if it is a tough situation between you and your family, spouse, best friend, at work, a decision you have faced with others or individually, or an illness. Whenever there is a disappointing or discouraging situation or need in your life, there are various ways to handle it. Nehemiah knew how to take the tough moments in his life to God in prayer and see them defined for God's glory! Nehemiah knew God was an ever-present source of help, and he was available to be used by God to faithfully do his part under very difficult circumstances. Disappointed and discouraged— not. Nehemiah was truly defined as a man of belief, contentment, and hope.

Nehemiah's Journey

Nehemiah was a man of prayer, faith, hope, and action. He knew where to turn when he was faced with a heart-crushing situation. Nehemiah was also willing to count the cost to see the Most High God's promises fulfilled. He was available to be used by God to accomplish His purposes in his lifetime. Nehemiah's life legacy reflected a life defined by dedication, resolve, and humility before God. His prayer life and his ability to motivate and encourage those around him flowed from his living relationship with the Almighty God. His personal life choices and daily focus were defined by God and not by his circumstances and environment. As you read the book of Nehemiah, you see Nehemiah wasn't only criticized, but was also bullied by his enemies, who made several attempts to make him look untrustworthy. Within Nehemiah's unique sphere of influence, his life choices were characterized by positive results. These results impacted not only his personal life but the lives of those around him. Nehemiah's influence affected his life and the lives of those around him in the areas of belief, restoration, contentment, and motivation. It restored joy of heart and soul based in their hope in the Everlasting God.

Nehemiah Chapters 1–2

Nehemiah was the cupbearer to King Artaxerxes of Persia. As cupbearer to the king, Nehemiah was placed in a position of great responsibility. Nehemiah's main responsibility was to taste the king's wine before he drank to ensure it hadn't been poisoned. This put Nehemiah in an intimate relationship with the king.

Nehemiah had received news from his Jewish brothers that the walls of the City of God, Jerusalem, were in disrepair. Nehemiah felt personal grief and heartbreak over this state of affairs. Nehemiah didn't allow the news or his circumstances to pull him down as he journeyed though the course of each day. The anguish and grief he felt, he immediately took to the throne of grace in prayer. The Sovereign God alone was his hope. Apart from God, Nehemiah knew that by his own efforts the city walls of Jerusalem couldn't be restored. Nehemiah was a man of prayer, who patiently acted on the convictions God laid within his heart.

Despite his heartbreak, Nehemiah's daily relationship and faith in God helped him face his storm. Nehemiah found peace with his sorrow by resting in God's provision and His Word. Over the course of your lifetime you may not have a deep conviction or opportunity to see actual city walls rebuilt and restored. However you will encounter circumstances that will crush your heart and grieve you to the core of your being that will require a rebuilding process in your life or the life of a loved one. You may have similar disappointing and discouraging thoughts and emotions like Nehemiah's. On your life journey, what has caused your thoughts and emotions to become defined by disappointment and discouragement?

The contexts of his journey and yours are different, but the similarities of heart and soul are the same. How do you respond to the crushing circumstances that come into your life? Do you immediately turn to God in prayer? Take time to read Nehemiah chapters 1 and 2, and listen to Nehemiah's heart, prayer, and surrender to God for circumstances he couldn't control. How does he trust the Almighty God to make him a part of the solution? How does Nehemiah move from disappointment to a strong belief and contentment founded in his hope in God? How did God provide and for whom?

Life's circumstances can either drain you or move you forward. Nehemiah knew his focus had to be on the Eternal God. As he prayed, Nehemiah reminds God time and again of the promises He made to His people over the ages. Pray to the God of heaven about what crushes your heart. He is listening and will hear you.

God sets a guard over your heart and life, and He will strengthen your hands and resolve to make it through those difficult moments of life, regardless of the circumstance that caused them. Find a Scripture passage that speaks to you about the circumstance or environment, and memorize it or read and reread it over, and over, and over again. When words escape you, pray God's promises from Scripture. In prayer and through God's promises, you will find strength, comfort, and a sustaining power to keep your focus on God. As a result, you will be defined by the Lord God Almighty and not by your circumstances or surroundings.

And I told them how the hand of my God had been favorable to me, and also about the king's words which he had spoken to me. Then they said, "Let us arise and build." So they put their hands to a good work. (Nehemiah 2:18)

One of the first animals we saw in Churchill was a red fox. As I think back on "Mr. Hollywood," he reminded me of Nehemiah and his ability to overcome the many obstacles he faced on his life journey. "Mr. Hollywood" was nestled down on the top of a huge gray rock along the shores of the Hudson Bay. The wind was fiercely blowing his fur, but he didn't seem to mind that at all. The temperature with the wind chill was extremely cold. My thought was, "Why not get down into the rocks and stay warm or go home?" For some reason, perhaps the vantage point or a determination to overcome the adverse circumstance or environment, "Mr. Hollywood" didn't appear to allow the events of his day to bother him a bit. We have much to learn from the animals that share our planet, as it is too easy for us to grumble in far less trying circumstances. Nehemiah was confident and determined despite the circumstance and environment that sought to distract and stop him from accomplishing his vision. You, too, can stand firm and overcome the obstacles you are facing.

Nehemiah's bond with the king was one of confidence, which would be beneficial to him in the future. During the days ahead as Nehemiah and the citizens of Jerusalem walked their journey together, their common bond would rest in their belief, hope, and faith in God. Not only did they trust God and seek Him to overcome their challenges, they worshipped His faithful presence and provision in their circumstances and the surroundings in which they found themselves each day.

Nehemiah Chapters 3–7

As the citizens of Jerusalem rebuilt the walls of the city, each individual built the portion in front of his or her own home. They had ownership of what they sought to accomplish. Being courageous and having a sense of control in one's life are helpful in maintaining a positive outlook and scattering the clouds of disappointment and discouragement. Unfortunately, this isn't always possible in the course of everyone's life. About the time you think you have life figured out, a Sanballat or Tobiah will come along and catch you off guard. They can quickly make you feel like you are falling into the canyon all over again. It may be a thought, a word, a memory, a person you see out of the blue that will cause you to feel like you are moving backward within your circumstance that surrounds you. Even though you feel like you are going backward, God knows everything that concerns you. Lift up the disappointment and discouragement to God, and allow Him to remove the darkness, sadness, and dust.

For Nehemiah, Sanballat and Tobiah are examples of individuals you might come into contact with who bring a critical, pessimistic view no matter what the topic might be. In this instance, they didn't desire the city's restoration and Nehemiah's commitment to this undertaking. Nehemiah's actions were most likely going to result in the failure of some of Sanballat and Tobiah's business investments. This was largely due to Nehemiah's appointment as governor over Jerusalem and the restoration project he was overseeing.

Sanballat and Tobiah were ancient-day bullies. When someone bullies you it attacks your self-confidence. At that point in time, you truly need to remind yourself who's child you are and who defines you. You are a child of the Most High God. And as the saying goes, "Sticks and stones may break my bones, but words will never hurt me." There are many times when those bullying others are really trying to build up their own self-esteem. The more insecure and discouraged they can make someone else feel results in them feeling more powerful and in control ... or so they think. In the long run, they end up hurting themselves. However, hurtful words and attitudes directed toward you at any level are upsetting and can remain painful for a lifetime. This is why it is important to rally around others close by and support each other in prayer. Fight the battle together, and seek the Lord Jesus Christ moment by moment. Cling to His side, and define yourself in His loving grace and mercy. You are a child of the Eternal King of all the ages, and He will walk with you through any canyon your life journey takes you. As you put one foot in front of the other you will be able to move forward and see change just like the citizens of Jerusalem did as they rebuilt their city walls.

I have always enjoyed the illustration about the glass being half full or half empty. I heard a gentleman provide a different twist on this phrase in that it also depends on the size of the glass. Sometimes our perspective on things is too narrow and self-absorbed. Other times we have a vision for what can be accomplished and dare to believe big things for and of God for ourselves and those around us, even as we encounter opposition. This is when the support, guidance, counsel, and prayers of others become critical to our survival! As we see in Nehemiah 2:10; 4:1–3; 6–8, when the battle intensified around the citizens of Jerusalem, they blew the trumpet, and others came to "rescue" and fight with them in the battle they were experiencing at the moment (Nehemiah 4:4–6; 9–23). It is important to surround yourself with family, friends, and in some instances, professional caregivers who will stand in the gap with you to provide guidance, prayer, and accountability. You weren't made to go it alone.

Our God will fight for us. (Nehemiah 4:20)

I will never desert you, nor will I ever forsake you. (Hebrews 13:5)

Many individuals are really good at camouflaging the deep feelings and concerns of their lives. You should never seek to fight your battle alone. Whatever wall you are tearing down or rebuilding in your life, it is okay to ask for help. The battles we confront throughout our life are many and varied. It may be the loss of a job or relationship, health concerns, the fact that your monthly budget is running short again, a conflict with a family member or friend (acquaintance, or boss) that you can't resolve, lies, addictions, fear of success, loneliness, mistakes that haunt you from actions taken, and so on. Maybe you are caught in an environment that is disrespectful, discriminating, bullying, or where illegal activities are carried out. Commit this area of your life to the Lord Jesus Christ in prayer by claiming a specific promise from God's Word. Your Father God delights in providing abundantly, beyond all your hopes and desires, as you surrender your heart and will to His guidance. He is awaiting your cry for help. And as you pray, remember to thank Jesus Christ for His continued faithfulness in every area of your life! Seeking professional counsel and the prayer support of others may be His means of helping you through the stormy seas. Thank Him for what He is teaching you through these difficult circumstances. God will provide for you in amazing ways. Look to Nehemiah's example of how he encouraged and directed others to rally around each other to see the difficulties overcome and the battle won. Surrounding yourself with those who love and support you is important when you are disappointed and discouraged. Having that common bond of fellowship in Christ is very important. God will refresh and restore you, bringing renewed belief, contentment, and hope for the days ahead.

As for me, I shall call upon God, And the Lord will save me. Evening and morning and at noon, I will complain and murmur, And He will hear my voice. He will redeem my soul in peace from the battle which is against me ... (Psalm 55:16–18)

Wait for the Lord; Be strong and let your heart take courage; Yes, wait for the Lord. (Psalm 27:14)

... My purpose will be established, And I will accomplish My good pleasure; (Isaiah 46:10)

As Nehemiah trusted the Most High God with this desperate need that had come into his life, he was able to patiently wait upon the Lord for His perfect timing to restore the inheritance of His people. By running to God in prayer, Nehemiah avoided the possibility of developing an anxious and critical spirit. He wasn't defined by his circumstances and environment. Prayer was Nehemiah's first defense toward making it through one of his life's difficult circumstances. He was defined by the God he trusted and relied on. He was a child of the Lord God Almighty, his Heavenly Father and Creator.

... But Thou art a God of forgiveness, Gracious and compassionate, Slow to anger, and abounding in lovingkindness; And Thou didst not forsake them. (Nehemiah 9:17)

Opposing forces will make you stronger and help you face the storms of your life journey. Just as the rocks in the stream bring music to the water as it flows downstream to its destination, so do the bumps in your road. The strength the bumps in the road develop will eventually bring music to your life, heart, and soul. The wind makes a tree stronger by causing its roots to grow deeper and stronger. I have always marveled at pine trees and flowers that grow on the mountainside. Somehow their roots have dug down deep and they are sustained to weather the storms they encounter where they are planted. God will help you to stand, just as He helped Nehemiah and the citizens of Jerusalem, even when you have nothing left to stand on or when you feel like you have nothing left inside you to give.

How blessed is the man who does not walk in the counsel of the wicked, Nor stand in the path of sinners, Nor sit in the seat of scoffers! But his delight is in the law of the Lord, And in His law he meditates day and night. And he will be like a tree firmly planted by the streams of water, Which yields its fruit in its season, And its leaf does not wither; And in whatever he does, he prospers. (Psalm 1:2-3)

Nehemiah Chapters 8–13

In the last chapters, we see Nehemiah, Ezra, and the citizens of Jerusalem reading the Word of God and worshipping the Lord. Their battle had ended. Through sweat and tears they made it through their difficult time. They had come together, prayed, and defended each other. And they saw God's faithfulness through His actions on their behalf. They remembered to take time to worship God and thank Him for all His blessings and provisions.

Commit your thoughts and desires to the Lord, and trust Him to work your circumstances out for good. When you trust God with the various circumstances and surroundings of your life, He may answer your prayer request with a yes, a no, or maybe even … wait. Your Heavenly Father's answer may not be what you expect, but God will act on your behalf based on what is the best for you and others. When God responds with a no to a prayer request, it may mean He has greater lessons to teach you or others who are also impacted by the specific prayer request. It may mean His protective hand is sparing you from something unforeseen that would have happened had He not shut the door. Remember, God is more concerned about your character and making you into His likeness than about your circumstances. And all things work together to bring glory to His name. Rest in Him, and trust in His sovereign timetable. Most of all seek to know Him with all your heart, delight to do His will, and then watch as He acts miraculously on your behalf for His glory! As you continue to seek God in prayer, your heart will also worship the God of the universe, who made you and created you for His pleasure. Bow down, seek His face, and humble yourself in His presence. Listen for His voice, and wait on Him; He will do it. The joy of the Lord is your strength!

Yet those who wait for the Lord will gain new strength; They will mount up with wings like eagles, They will run and not get tired, They will walk and not become weary. (Isaiah 40:31)

Cease striving and know that I am God; I will be exalted among the nations, I will be exalted in the earth. (Psalm 46:10)

... Do not be grieved, for the joy of the Lord
is your strength. (Nehemiah 8:10)

Hope in Christ and His provision. He is the answer to help you overcome being defined by the circumstances of life that create disappointment and discouragement. Those who are able to shake the dust and overcome these things are willing to look beyond the circumstance, and choose not to allow these feelings to control how they are defined. They have learned how to be content in their circumstances. They believe that despite the "mess" that they or a loved one are in, God will be glorified, and He will provide a better outcome. You, too, need to choose not to become focused and absorbed by disappointing circumstances, which will eventually lead to discouragement. You need to confidently choose to live and be defined by belief, contentment, and hope.

As with Nehemiah, your battle is won together with your trusted brothers and sisters in Christ. Allow them to walk and support you in your journey. Together, rejoice in what God has done. Rejoice in the unknown conclusions of your yesterdays, rejoice in the hurtful moments of today, rejoice and celebrate the moments of your life that make no sense—whether they happened today or ten to fifteen years ago. And rejoice in your tomorrows, knowing your Lord and Savior, Jesus Christ, will be there to sustain and enfold you in His abundant light, mercy, grace, and careful provision. God's great love for you stands in the gaps of your unfulfilled expectations and the healing that may not happen. He stands victorious in a world that is at war with His purposes and righteousness. You are a child of the Most High God—the Lord Jesus Christ. He is holy and reigns over all, and He cares for you, regardless of where your journey has taken you! Shake the dust of weariness, regret, pride, resentment, deceit, disappointment, discouragement, envy, anger, bitterness, defeat, and anything else affecting you, and walk in the light of today with a grateful heart. Rest in His love and peace, knowing His purpose and restored joy; living with honesty, integrity, and selflessness; sustained by your faith in God; being firmly rooted in your beliefs; content in Christ; and filled with His hope for today and tomorrow. Know true happiness, peace, trust, and the pure love and light of God found only in Jesus Christ.

God prepares the way before you each day. Nehemiah had a close relationship with the Lord. Despite his conflicts, trials, and daily hassles he encountered, Nehemiah refused to allow or be defined by these negative circumstances. He didn't allow them to rob him of the joy he had in knowing he was one of God's chosen children. His daily circumstances weren't always easy. He was stretched and challenged on his journey. However, he was victorious, because he knew the Sovereign God, his Heavenly Father, the Lord God Almighty, had faithfully prepared the way before him. Nehemiah had others walking alongside him in his journey who pointed him back to God when the going got bumpy. Together they were stronger and could support each other through the difficult times. Nehemiah knew how to trust, listen, and obey. And he was good at thanking God for His provision by claiming God's promise in prayer. Nehemiah worshipped and glorified his God in recognition of all His faithfulness and blessings bestowed on him.

For Further Thought

What circumstances/environment do you see in Nehemiah's life that challenged his walk with God? How did he handle this circumstances/environment in his life?

What resources did Nehemiah rely on?

How did God/Jesus Christ act on his behalf?

What lessons can you learn from Nehemiah's life journey?

How did this circumstance/environment define Nehemiah's character?

How can you apply these lessons to your life or a friend's?

My study of Nehemiah prompts me to trust God for _____, _____, and _____. I will _____ in order to trust God more completely with this circumstance/environment in my life.

David's Journey with Goliath

David is defined as a man after God's own heart. This is an awesome legacy to have, considering David's résumé included job opportunities such as shepherd, musician, warrior, and king. He was a responsible man: a husband, a father, and loyal friend. When you look closely at David's life, you will see he wasn't a perfect man by any means. David also made some unwise choices in his life journey, such as committing adultery and murder (2 Samuel 11–12). However, David's heart was quick to turn toward repentance and humility before humankind and before the Sovereign God, whom he worshipped and honored throughout his lifetime. His relationship with God was daily and real through the good and the bad times of his life journey.

1 Samuel 17:1–16

As you read chapter 17 of 1 Samuel, the Philistines have gathered against the armies of Israel for battle. The armies of Israel were taunted on a daily basis by a Philistine warrior and became dismayed and greatly afraid (1 Samuel 17:11). Their fear had stopped them dead in their tracks. They were paralyzed and defined by the fear of the unknown. The words of mockery and shame showered upon them in arrogance and disrespect left them discouraged and disappointed. Their army was unable to fight against the Philistines in battle, and they were unable to take a stand and take action in a difficult circumstance. Their circumstance and environment were having a direct impact on their future. Have you ever been there? Afraid of what might unfold for the future? Unsure of how to take action in a situation that not only intimidated you could result in even greater difficulties for you, your family, or those you hold dear to your heart.

1 Samuel 17:17–25

David's father sent him to the battlefield to take provisions and supplies to his brothers. The army of Israel was engaged in an ongoing battle with the Philistines. David had visited the battlefield on many occasions, but this time it was different. When David arrived, he found a very perplexing battle going on. Daily, a very large man, a Philistine named Goliath, taunted the armies of Israel and the Lord God Almighty. Morning and evening for forty days, Goliath hurled insult after insult toward the armies of Saul. As a result of their choices, Saul, the king of Israel, and his army were cowering before Goliath and his bullying words. King Saul and his army had lost their vision. They weren't only ineffective, they were unable to take action in order to subdue their enemy at any level. David's encounter with the Philistine "giant," Goliath, is a life lesson for each of us on many levels.

1 Samuel 17:27–37

Once young David arrived, he began asking questions about what was going on. "For who is this uncircumcised Philistine, that he should taunt the armies of the living God?" (1 Samuel 17:26). His brothers, upset about his inquiring mind, questioned his motives and why he was really there. David soon discovered there would be a reward for anyone who would fight the giant on behalf of Israel. David wasn't concerned about the reward, but he was concerned about the army of Israel, and the Philistine who was taunting the Lord God Almighty, the Sovereign God of the universe. David's faith stated it plainly: this guy shouldn't be bullying us nor taunting the Living God! David was basically saying, "Who does this man Goliath think he is anyway? I will take him on!"

How do you make pivotal decisions for your life—out of faith or fear? What defines those critical moments in your life? How does the power of the Holy Spirit provide you with the endurance to persevere through the circumstance and environment that surround you? Do you know the strength, mercy, and grace of God's character and provision that are available to you every moment of every day?

For I am convinced that neither death, nor life, nor angels, nor principalities, nor things present, nor things to come, nor powers, nor height, nor depth, nor any other created thing, shall be able to separate us from the love of God, which is in Christ Jesus our Lord. (Romans 8:38–39)

1 Samuel 17:38–40

David volunteered to fight Goliath on behalf of the armies of King Saul. King Saul encased David in his armor to prepare him for battle. Picture a young man dressed in an adult man's suit of armor. Possibly the helmet sits so low on his head that it covers David's eyes, the breastplate hangs to his knees, and Saul's shield is hard to lift and carry. David was now encumbered with what his world determined to be the appropriate tools for the battle of a lifetime. So what did David do? He took off the armor and picked up the tools of his trade: his shepherd's stick and five smooth stones from the nearby brook. He placed them prayerfully into his shepherd's bag, took his sling, and approached Goliath.

Then David said to the Philistine, "You come to me, with a sword, a spear, and a javelin, but I come to you in the name of the Lord of hosts, the God of the armies of Israel, whom you have taunted. "This day the Lord will deliver you up into my hands, and I will strike you down and remove your head from you … that all the earth may know that there is a God in Israel, and that all this assembly may know that the Lord does not deliver by sword or by spear; for the battle is the Lord's and He will give you into our hands." (1 Samuel 17:45–47)

1 Samuel 17:41–51

Of course, Goliath was greatly insulted and filled with disdain at the fact the army of Israel sent a ruddy youth to fight him. Goliath's mockery and bullying of David's choice of battle gear (sticks and stones) was intense. And his arrogant pride that he, the great Goliath, would be more than happy to feed David's body to the birds of the air and the beasts of the field were strongly proclaimed. But David knew his Sovereign God, and he knew God would fight on his behalf that day. David knew God would be honored and glorified through the victory God would give them that day.

1 Samuel 17:52–58

David and Nehemiah both experienced being bullied. Unfortunately, being taunted or bullied is something most of us go through, at some point, in our life journey. It is a painful place to be. It can be demoralizing or empowering, depending on what your focus rests on. In David's case, Goliath was taunting the foundation of his faith and belief system. He was also personally taunted and bullied because of his choice of battle gear. But David focused on the facts and who his Eternal God is, was, and will be. And he knew God had trained and equipped him with the gear he brought to the battle. He wasn't afraid; he was confident in who his Heavenly Father created him to be.

Because of David's faith-based beliefs, contentment, rest, and hope in the Almighty God, the battle was won! He didn't allow negative thoughts—his own or those of others—to weigh him down. David rose above the attitudes and fears that surrounded him. He shook off the dust of the worn and broken pieces that could have dragged him down and cause him to lose the joy God provided for him in his life journey. The same holds true for you and for me. David was defined by his Creator God. He didn't allow King Saul and Goliath's battle strategy to define who he was: young, inexperienced, untrained, and so on. David approached life through prayer with confidence and security in the Lord God Almighty. His example teaches us the importance of being yourself as you walk your life journey by using the tools and gifts God has given you for His service to others and for His glory. God is honored as you rest and hope in Him to accomplish His purposes. Remember, as David rested and hoped in the Lord's provision, he was also taking a stand and taking action to see a resolution to the battle/circumstance/environment that had presented itself that day.

Finally, be strong in the Lord, and in the strength of His might. Put on the full armor of God, that you may be able to stand firm against the schemes of the devil. For our struggle is not against flesh and blood, but against the rulers, against the powers, against the world forces of this darkness, against the spiritual forces of wickedness in the heavenly places. Therefore take up the full armor of God, that you may be able to resist in the evil day, and having done everything to stand firm. Stand firm therefore having girded your loins with truth, and having put on the breastplate of righteousness, and having shod your feet with the preparation of the gospel of peace; in addition to all, taking up the shield of faith with which you will be able to extinguish all the flaming missiles of the evil one. And take the helmet of salvation, and the sword of the Spirit, which is the word of God. (Ephesians 6:10–17)

For Further Thought

What circumstance/environment do you see in David's life that challenged his walk with God? How did he handle this circumstance/environment in his life?

What resources did David rely on?

How did God/Jesus Christ act on his behalf?

What lessons can you learn from David's life journey?

How did this circumstance/environment define David's character?

How can you apply these lessons to your life or a friend's?

My study of David and Goliath prompts me to trust God for

_____ , _____ , and

_____ . I will _____ in
order to trust God more completely with this circumstance/
environment in my life.

A Lesson from a Polar Bear
Hope—Hebrews 11:1
Be Inquisitive and Strong, and Persevere

One polar bear we saw on our journey was very precious. She
was inquisitive, sniffing out her new friends, getting a good
look at the tundra buggy wheels and tracks, and peering in the
windows to see what type of creatures were making clicking
sounds (cameras) and wonderful sounds of joy and laughter. Life
is full of discoveries. Many events in life cause us to look at
things very differently and require hope, extra strength, and
perseverance of ourselves and those we love in order to see a new
beginning. The power of the human spirit is amazing.

As I watched a biblically based series on the Old and New
Testaments, aired by the History Channel, I was silenced by Christ's
perseverance to carry His cross and move, with determination,
toward the crucifixion. May you draw on the knowledge that
Christ has experienced and understands all you think and feel
each day. Continue to ask Him for the ability to approach each
new day with a sense of inquisitiveness about how He will work

on your behalf. Ask Him to continue to sustain you and give you strength and perseverance for whatever lies ahead. Jesus always stands in the gap. All you need to do is cry to Him, even if all you can muster is the word "Help."

6 Shaking the Dust of Envy, Anger, Bitterness, and Defeat - Defined by Happiness, Peace, and Trust

The Lord is compassionate and gracious, Slow to anger and abounding in lovingkindness. He will not always strive with us; Nor will He keep His anger forever. He has not dealt with us according to our sins, Nor rewarded us according to our iniquities. For as high as the heavens are above the earth, So great is His lovingkindness toward those who fear Him. As far as the east is from the west, So far has He removed our transgressions from us. Just as the father has compassion on his children, So the Lord has compassion on those who fear Him. For He Himself knows our frame; He is mindful that we are but dust.

—*Psalm 103:8–14*

Circumstances and environments that define who you are can originate from external events and decisions or from those you can control. Jonah saw God work a huge miracle in turning the hearts of a godless nation to God through the message of repentance, which he preached in the streets of Nineveh, only to find himself orchestrating his own pity party because he didn't like God's outcome. Joseph, on the other hand, as a youth and young adult was dealt a hand that wasn't fair and honest, and was less than desirable. Joseph lived above his circumstances and surroundings and didn't allow them to define who he was. One can continually observe in Joseph's life—despite the circumstances of his life journey—a pursuit of commitment, integrity, and service for others.

Ruth stepped out in faith, followed her mother-in-law in devotion and love, and committed to live with Naomi's people. Ruth accepted a personal relationship with the Lord God Almighty as a result of Naomi's influence in her life. Ruth saw something that defined Naomi and determined that it was worth clinging to through her own life journey. Their initial return to Israel wasn't easy, but through faith and trust, God provided abundantly for their needs, beyond what they could have ever dreamed possible. God honored Ruth's words and actions, which were backed by trust, hope, and faith in the Almighty God.

David and Bathsheba's Journey

There is the possibility of us forgetting the individuals who have their journeys documented for us in the Bible are truly human beings, just like you and me. They lived, breathed, and walked on earth, and "put their pants on one leg at a time." They had feelings of joy and hope, as well as feelings of utter desperation and deep grief. They laughed, cried, sang, danced, became angry, and made right and wrong choices on their life journeys. David and Bathsheba were no exception.

Taking a bird's-eye view of David and his first meeting with Bathsheba will help us to see how David continued to define his life and actions, good and bad, in the Lord God Almighty. His actions shouldn't encourage us to make unwise choices. But his example can teach us how to redefine self-inflicted circumstances and environments.

What shall we say then? Are we to continue in sin that grace might increase? May it never be! (Romans 6:1–2)

2 Samuel 11:1–17

In chapter 5, we looked at David's encounter with the Philistine, Goliath. To this day, David's legacy has defined him as a man after God's own heart (1 Kings 3:14; 11:38; 14:7–8). However, in the account of David's life found in 2 Samuel, David is following his own lustful desires, taking what wasn't rightfully his (committing adultery with Bathsheba), and then manipulating his military directives to create an opportunity where Uriah, Bathsheba's husband, would be killed (murdered) on the front lines of the battlefield. David's actions of looking, inquiring, and taking Bathsheba were the result of unwise choices (2 Samuel 11:1–5). His actions continued to spiral him downward into one of the deepest canyons of his life. At approximately fifty years old, David's choices found him involved in covering up his sinful actions, practicing deceit and manipulation, and then taking the life of an innocent and honorable man (2 Samuel 11:6–17).

When you realize you have sinned and taken the wrong direction in life, it most likely will not be easy to turn the boat around midstream. But acknowledge the wrong, and seek to make things right if it is in your power to do so. Seek legal and/or medical counsel and help if necessary. Seek the guidance of a wise friend who will come alongside to help you fight the enemies encircling you. Petition Jesus Christ fervently in prayer, and don't let go. Jesus Christ will be there in the darkness and will meet you exactly where you are. He loves you and will not let go. Shake off the dust of the envy, anger, bitterness, and defeat that seek to encrust your being. Rest in His almighty, nail-pierced hand, and cling to His pierced side. Jesus Christ died and rose from the dead to restore you to a right relationship with your Father. Cry out to Him, and He will restore the broken pieces of your worn life. In Him you will find the wonder of His happiness, peace, and a trusting relationship that will endure for all eternity! "… But with God all things are possible." (Matthew 19:26).

But the salvation of the righteous is from the Lord; He is their strength in time of trouble. And the Lord helps them, and delivers them; He delivers them from the wicked, and saves them, Because they take refuge in Him. (Psalm 37:39–40)

2 Samuel 11:26–12:1–23

In reading the above scripture, you see David being confronted about his sin by Nathan, the prophet. David recognizes his sinful actions, repents, and humbles himself before God through fasting and fervent prayer. He prays his newborn child with Bathsheba would be spared. Later, through the hushed conversations of those around him, David found out the child had passed away. "So David arose from the ground, washed, and anointed himself, and changed his clothes; he came into the house of the Lord and worshipped … " (2 Samuel 12:20). David's response to those observing his actions revealed, "while the child was still alive, I fasted and wept; for I said, 'Who knows, the Lord may be gracious to me, that the child might live. But now he has died; why should I fast? Can I bring him back again? I shall go to him, but he will not return to me.' Then David comforted his wife, Bathsheba ..." (2 Samuel 12:22–24).

Did David and Bathsheba have regrets, shed tears? Did they miss the child they lost? Did they ever wonder why this happened or what could have been? David and Bathsheba were flesh and blood, just like you and me, so they probably did. Were they able to look at God's tapestry of their lives and see the beautiful image on the front of their tangled thread weaving? Just like you, they didn't know the end result.

Tragedy comes to our lives in many ways during our life journey. God isn't cruel, heartless, or unfair. Nor is He is out to "get you" or make your life miserable. He is just in all of His actions, His reasoning is all-knowing, and His perspective is greater than yours. He doesn't expect you to understand His ways, but He does desire you to trust, obey, and seek Him in every circumstance of your life. Are there circumstances in your life that will continue to tug at your heartstrings over the course of your life journey when you least expect it? Will you feel a sense of pain, sorrow, possible regrets and/or a sense of hopelessness? It is possible, but at those unexpected moments, turn those feelings over to your Heavenly Father, who will take and heal them in your heart and mind. Life journey circumstances may never make complete sense to you, but this doesn't impact or change God's purposes and intentions of extravagant grace, mercy, and love toward you. He hears your every whispered sigh and cares deeply and intimately about you.

The past is behind you, and you can't change what has already happened. Maybe actions toward restoration need to take place, maybe words of apology need to be said, maybe you need to forgive yourself and let the past go and move on. Don't be tempted to beat yourself up over whatever circumstances you have allowed to define who you are. Prayerfully seek change for today, and move toward changing your future. God has moved in love and power through His Son Jesus Christ to restore you yesterday, today, and tomorrow. Whatever it is that you have done, God in His infinite love has forgiven you. The sin is gone, and you have been made new in Jesus Christ. David trusted in the loving hand of God and His righteousness, and his life was made new. David could have become angry and bitter over the death of this son. David experienced God's forgiveness washing over him and knew his God had restored and made him clean. David's sins were forgiven and forever forgotten by His Heavenly Father. God has also forgiven your confessed sin through Jesus Christ's shed blood. David acknowledged God's rightful place in his life and accepted God's perfect oversight over the details of his life. Trust in Him!

Shortly after the death of this child, David and Bathsheba had a special gift from God, a new son, Solomon who one day would become king.

Consider it all joy, my brethren, when you encounter various trials, knowing that the testing of your faith produces endurance. And let endurance have its perfect result, that you may be perfect and complete, lacking in nothing. But if any of you lacks wisdom, let him ask of God, who gives to all men generously and without reproach, and it will be given to him. But let him ask in faith without any doubting, for the one who doubts is like the surf of the sea driven and tossed by the wind. (James 1:2–6)

Moving beyond the known and expected framework of your life will take a conscientious effort. Circumstances that result in a premature "death" by creating a change of direction are hard to accept and understand. It doesn't matter if the death is physical (regardless of the age of the person) or if it is the death of a dream, relationship, activity, or anything else. Letting go of the loss—person or thing—may take every ounce of your energy to accomplish. And in the long run, it will only be overcome by abiding in the Lord Jesus Christ. Allow Him to redefine the loss, and He will help you climb up the canyon trail to the crest of the valley, where you will be able to continue to move forward in the light of His grace, mercy, and love. Allow Him to take your losses in life regardless of the circumstance or environment, and allow Him to use this time of loss to draw you closer to His side. Trust in His mysteries, and watch and ask Him to show you how He will bring good out of the bad that has unfolded in your life.

Remember, you are always as close to His side as you can possibly be. He is your Lord God, your Everlasting Father. In times of cold and chilly darkness, when you need to shake the dusty ice crystals,

He may seem even closer than when things are going smoothly in your life. Rest in the palm of His hand, stay close to His heart, and listen for His grace and mercy in the dark stillness. Know that no matter how rough and bumpy it becomes, He understands and is there walking and carrying you forward with each breath you take. Will some days be better than others? Yes. Will some days be the total pits? Yes they will.

In the polar bear I saw a purposeful peace amid the harshness of its environment. The polar bear's need to move out onto the sea ice for the long and dark winter was urgent, for it is there it finds its main source of food. His approach to the wintery journey ahead appeared to be timeless, and there was no rush. God created the polar bear to be strong, massive, silent, persistent, observant, enchanting, inquisitive, mysterious, methodical, whimsical, and resourceful. Therefore, God prepared the polar bear to be ready for the exacting journey ahead. Just like the polar bear and David, you may stand strong and purposeful in your life journey.

The storms of life can leave you feeling dirty and downtrodden. To me, the polar bear's fur was washed as white as the snow surrounding it. You, too, are washed as white as snow by the hand of God and prepared in Christ for whatever your life journey brings your way. Talk to Jesus about how you feel, and ask Him to fill the void within you that has been created by this circumstance or environment. Step out and trust God to make you a new person in Christ.

Wash yourselves, make yourselves clean; Remove the evil of your deeds from My sight. Cease to do evil, Learn to do good; Seek justice, Reprove the ruthless; Defend the orphan, Plead for the widow. "Come now, and let us reason together," Says the Lord, "Though your sins are as scarlet, They will be as white as snow; Though they are red like crimson, They will be like wool." (Isaiah 1:16–18)

As you have observed, your life journey will be impacted by circumstances—positive or negative—beyond your control or by events/actions of your own orchestration. These circumstances will not only impact your life but may also impact the lives of others. By making a choice to leave the bad attitude, the disappointment, the death of a vision/dream, or the death of a loved one, or to embrace an illness, and so on, you will find your life has become what many have coined as the new normal. Things are different, and they may not be what they had been or what you dreamed they would be. However, you may rise above the circumstance and environment of pride, resentment, deceit, disappointment, discouragement, regret, envy, anger, bitterness, just like David did. And you can trust God to make your new normal a new and special blessing every day. Seek to praise Him and bring glory to God through the devastation, whatever the cause. Know that He loves you with an everlasting love. You are a child of the Sovereign God of all ages. He is your Heavenly Father, and you are defined by His light and love. In due time, happiness, peace, and trust will be restored as you trust God with the big and small details throughout your life journey.

Moving forward and living outside your comfort box or routine is difficult. There may be choices that you need to make that will not quite fit what you have been use to in your life journey. You may need to accept God's release to leave your past and the familiar behind, and that can be very difficult. Maybe you are in need of closure, and it is not coming as you had hoped or expected. Your emotions may be overwhelming as the stormy waters buffet you from all sides.

From my distress I called upon the Lord; The Lord answered me and set me in a large place. The Lord is for me; and I will not fear; What can man do to me? (Psalm 118:5–6)

As I left the fog of my caregiving days and the death of my mother, I found it very hard at times to rest in the happiness and peaceful joy God was restoring in my life. It was easier to hide in my comfort box of the past and the pain and sorrow that had filled my days after her death. During the last few years of her life, it was easy to help her move into her new normal. But I struggled with moving into my own new normal after her eternal homecoming. My mom loved to go on walks. When she was unable to walk, we "walked" to the nearby park via wheelchair. When she could no longer handle the customers at the ice cream shop, the ice cream came to her. When she no longer understood what church was about, through my tears, I prayed harder and reminded her that God's love surrounded and cared for her. Prayer sustained us both in the new normals of each moment of each new day. By remaining in my comfort box after her death, I felt like I was going to keep her memory and her alive longer.

In reality, I was silently moving into the darkness that would define my character in a manner God didn't desire for me as His precious child. It is often easier to believe things for others than for ourselves. God works just as powerfully in your life as He does within your family, as He does in your best friend's life, and in the individuals who live halfway around the world. Be open to God's lead and take His hand. Hold tightly, and move one foot in front of the other. Keep your focus on Him, and pray through your emotions and circumstances every minute of your day or night if you need to. He is always listening and is never bored or bothered by listening to your struggles or confusion. Bring your complaints and thanksgivings to His throne of grace and mercy for His ongoing presence and care in your life. Find new ways to enjoy the things that are meaningful to you, your family, or for others. Learn to live in the moment, and seek out your Creator God's special blessings just for you. Learn to rest in His happiness, peace, and trusting relationship.

Keep yourselves in the love of God, ... (Jude 1:21)

I met a weathered and delightful rancher who was usually attired in his work clothes: custom drooped cowboy hat, scarf, chaps, and spurs. One day I smiled as he commented, "There are clouds coming over the mountain. Maybe if we are blessed they will bring us some rain. And when the rain comes, we will thank the Lord." Having weathered an E-3 tornado, I often look at the clouds and also hope for rain. Unfortunately, I tend to focus on the potential of the storm's thunder, lightning, wind, and rain that may come and become fearful of what might happen between the ground and sky. Too often we focus on the storms of life when we should focus on the blessing of the rain and thank God regardless of the outcome. Jesus Christ was with you before and during the storm, and He will be faithful to guide and provide whatever your needs may be after the storm. Circumstances and environment, as you have discovered, should never define who you are. Of all the things that you might fear in life, of all the things that you might and can lose in life, you can never lose the Lord Jesus Christ. He is forever faithful. He is your Lord and Savior yesterday, today, and forever!

Trust and allow yourself to be dependent on the Lord God with all the outcomes of your life. Tune your heart to the Lord. When you are confronted with an unpleasant TV or radio station, you tune the station to make it acceptable. With some "stations" in your life, once you have changed the channel, you will need to leave that tuning button alone! Don't turn it back to see what happens next or, in many instances, what the reason was for the pain or suffering that occurred. In some situations, however, looking back could prove to be beneficial, depending on the circumstance or environment. In some situations, it may be appropriate for you to seek safety, counsel, guidance, restoration, or forgiveness. He will be faithful to guide and lead you in the minutes and days ahead. Listen to the godly counsel of friends and professional caregivers. Your Lord God is with you and will fight your battle for and with you if you let Him. The Holy Spirit will strengthen you throughout your life journey. Return home to His extravagant and everlasting love, mercy, grace, and peace. He is always waiting with open arms.

Life moves on, and God doesn't desire for you to be caught and defined by a web of sorrow, bitterness, regret, and discouragement. It is okay to feel grief, disappointment, discouragement, and so on, in your life journey. These are all part of being human. But to camp in these negative moments and to not trust in the Lord God Almighty's powerful hand to walk you out of the darkness, isn't His intention for you. Walk with the Lord Jesus Christ, and allow Him to lead you into the warmth of His glorious light, love, forgiveness, and joy. You are God's child—the child of the Most High. David made mistakes, he acknowledged them, and he moved on. David's heart, soul, and character remained firmly defined in God's love and purpose for his life. Just as God loved David in all of his humanness, so He loves you because of who He is. And God's love, for you, is secure for all eternity. In trust, hope, faith, and obedience, David's life continued to move forward. He and Bathsheba had a new normal, and they moved triumphantly forward in the power of the Holy Spirit.

Trust in the Lord with all your heart, And do not lean on your own understanding. In all your ways acknowledge Him, And He will make your paths straight. (Proverbs 3:5–6)

For Further Thought

What circumstances/environments do you see in David's and Bathsheba's lives that challenged their walks with God? How did they handle their circumstances/environments?

What resources did David and Bathsheba rely on?

How did God/Jesus Christ act on their behalf?

What lessons can you learn from David's and Bathsheba's life journeys?

How did these circumstances/environments define David's and Bathsheba's characters?

How can you apply these lessons to your life or a friend's?

My study of David and Bathsheba prompts me to trust God for _____, _____, and _____. I will _____ in order to trust God more completely with this circumstance/environment in my life.

A Lesson from a Polar Bear
Trust—Psalm 23
Sniff out What the Day Has in Store

The polar bears that befriended us on our Churchill journey were by themselves. The only thing we could hear as we watched the bears was their sniffing the air to try to figure out who we were. They were direct and methodical in their approach to determining what had changed in their environment. Once they determined we weren't a threat to them, they went about their life, confident in the outcome of what was ahead for them in the days and weeks ahead. May you allow God to grant you the grace and ability to sniff out (discern) what each day has in store for you. There will be ups and downs, joys and sorrows, but know the Lord God Almighty has walked ahead of you and knows every inch of the path that lies ahead for you. He will guide and protect you and bring blessings along the way that will lighten your load and bring you confidence in His power and mercy to provide His very best for you.

7 Shaking the Dust of Life's Journey - Defined by Love - the Love of Jesus Christ

There is an appointed time for everything.
And there is a time for every event under heaven -
A time to give birth, and a time to die;
A time to plant; and a time to uproot what is planted.
A time to kill, and a time to heal;
A time to tear down, and a time to build up.
A time to weep, and a time to laugh;
A time to mourn, and a time to dance.
A time to throw stones, and a time to gather stones;
A time to embrace, and a time to shun embracing.
A time to search, and a time give up as lost;
A time to keep, and a time to throw away.
A time to tear apart, and a time to sew together;
A time to be silent, and a time to speak.
A time to love, and a time to hate;
A time for war, and a time for peace.
—Ecclesiastes 3:1–8

You are the Most Holy God's son or daughter. You are beyond precious in His sight. Your Heavenly Father, Creator God, formed you in His image. You have the ability to discover, create, laugh, feel pain and sorrow, and cry. You are human, and the varied emotions you feel and experience are normal on your life journey.

These emotions can build your character and make you a stronger person, or as the saying goes, they can "eat you alive!" There is a time for every purpose under heaven—to be disappointed, to feel regret, to mourn, to encounter sickness or the inability to do something you enjoy, to lose something dear to your heart, to experience fear and anxiety, and so on. All these emotions, thoughts, and circumstances are perfectly normal and will be a part of your life journey. However, to allow your emotions and feelings to control and take over your thoughts, heart, and soul, or to consume your day-to-day existence is not your Father's desire for your life.

As you seek God's face through the stormy circumstances and surroundings of your life journey, remember the life principles you have studied from God's Word, and follow them daily. Allow brothers and sisters in Christ to encourage and remind you that God's care and purpose for your life are secure. As I have trusted the Lord in my life journey, I have seen a growth in my own life, as Jesus and I have walked hand in hand (and often He has carried me through the rising waters, wind, and fire). I have seen my character defined by His plan and purposes and not my own. If I had camped in one of those hurtful spots, the growth and healing process completed by the Holy Spirit's seeds of faith, hope, and peace wouldn't have been able to grow and mature. Without the Lord Jesus Christ and His tools of mercy throwing me a lifeline, I would have swallowed a lot of water in the stormy seas. The emotions and thoughts you have are a normal part of life when expressed in prayer with the One who loves you the most, Jesus Christ. He will heal and restore your heart and soul, so you are defined by His love and not by the things that can encumber and pull you down. God needs your willing heart. He doesn't need you to be perfect. Live above the moment, and make choices that lead to God-filled intentions for each moment of each day.

Are you or a friend currently in an emotional or spiritual desert or a physical wilderness of silence and darkness? Changing your behavior and thoughts begin with Jesus Christ changing your heart. Like the Prodigal Son run back to God your Father. Believe Almighty God, and give Him control of your life. Allow Him to redefine your life purpose and be an overcomer of the circumstances and environments that seek to defeat you. Choose not to live a defeated life by learning how to trust God moment by moment each day. Lay your desires, burdens, and dusty broken pieces down at the foot of the cross of Jesus Christ. Draw on the strength and power of the Holy Spirit so that you can see His multitude of blessings each day! (Remember, blessings don't always equal places, things, people, money, success, and so on.) Diligently pursue time with Him daily, and talk to Him constantly if necessary. Talk with God like you would your best friend. He is closer than a breath away. Confide and abide always in Him. Your focus must remain on your Lord and Savior Jesus Christ and His great love, mercy, and grace for you through all of the battlefields your life journey will take you through. You will experience sorrow and frustrations, you will experience anger and pain, you will experience joy and laughter, and you will experience peace and rest. All these emotions and thoughts need to be in balance and surrounded by God's loving care and protection for you through the power and wisdom of His Holy Spirit. God will never abandon you. His love for you is unconditional and unending! Place your confidence in Jesus Christ. Ask God to remind you who you are in His eyes. Come back to the Lord God Almighty and run to His open arms. He is waiting for you to come to Him and seek His face. You are His child!

And He said, "A certain man had two sons; and the younger of them said to his father, 'Father give me the share of the estate that falls to me.' And he divided his wealth between them. And not many days later, the younger son gathered everything together and went on a journey into a distant country, and there he squandered his estate with loose living. Now when he had spent everything, a severe famine occurred in the country, and he began to be in need. And he went and attached himself to one of the citizens of the country, and he sent him into his fields to feed swine. And he was longing to fill his stomach with the pods that the swine were eating, and no one was giving him anything to him. But when he came to his senses, he said 'How many of my father's hired men have more than enough bread, but I am dying here with hunger! I will get up and go to my father, and will say to him, "Father, I have sinned against heaven, and in your sight; I am no longer worthy to be called your son; make me as one of your hired men."' And he got up and came to his father. But while he was still a long way off, his father saw him, and felt compassion for him, and ran and embraced him, and kissed him. "And the son said to him, 'Father I have sinned against heaven and in your sight; I am no longer worthy to be called your son.' But the father said to his slaves, 'Quickly bring out the best robe and put it on him, and put a ring on his hand and sandals on his feet; and bring the fattened calf, kill it, and let us eat and be merry; for this son of mine was dead, and has come to life again; he was lost, and has been found.' And they began to be merry. ... "But we had to be merry and rejoice, for this brother of yours was dead and has begun to live, and was lost and has been found.'" (Luke 15:11–24, 32)

Exodus 14:13–31

As you have seen, the Lord God Almighty is your strength and refuge in the all the storms your life will encounter. Consider the parting of the Red Sea as the Israelites passed across on dry ground safe and secure, as the Egyptians nipped at their heels, so to speak. This Scripture passage reminds you of several of God's promises. The magnificent God we serve is always faithful and true. He protected and cared for the His children's every need as they left the slavery of Egypt. He will always do the same for you. As they left Egypt and entered the Promised Land and crossed the Red Sea, no one was harmed. No one got wet or even stuck in the mud! As God's children, we need to pursue four things. *Trust*—trust in the Lord God Almighty. *Hope and Faith*—"Keep on keeping on," as the phrase goes. Keep putting one foot in front of the other despite what circumstances may tell you or how you may feel; keep moving forward. Be smart about how you move forward. Seek legal or medical counsel when necessary. Seek the guidance of a Pastor or trusted family member or friend. There are often circumstances you were never meant to walk alone. *Obey*—don't look back. Focus on Jesus. He will do it; He will save you. Maybe not in the fashion you expected, but He will take perfect care of you on your entire life journey. From your first earthly baby breath to the last tearful sigh, He will take your hand and lead you into heavenly eternity!

> Tune your anxious heart to patience, walk by faith where sight is dim; loving God, be calm and trustful. And leave everything to Him. (Oswald Chambers, evangelist and teacher, AD 1874–AD 1917)

As the Israelites crossed the Red Sea, they needed to remember to not look back. Unfortunately, at times they loudly complained about what they had left behind in Egypt. Don't lose sight that the shadows of your life bring tears of blessing! They were headed toward a new normal, a new life journey with their Lord God Almighty leading the way. Remember, don't look to the right or left. Look up, straight ahead, with a fixed focus directly to the Lord Jesus Christ. You will go out in joy. You will be led forth in peace. Place your hope in Jesus Christ, and remember to thank Him for what He is has done and what He is about to do on your behalf.

> *O Lord, Thou art my God; I will exalt Thee, I will give thanks to Thy name; For Thou hast worked wonders, Plans formed long ago, with perfect faithfulness. (Isaiah 25:1)*

Just like the Israelites leaving Egypt, as you pursue the Lord's new definition for your life, you will have moments of hope alongside moments of disbelief and discouragement. There will be seasons where shattered dreams may be sprinkled with possible regret.

You may experience anger. Lift these honest emotions to the Lord in prayer, and ask for His rest and peace. Don't allow mistrust, bitterness, or a "poor me" attitude to take root. Run from any sign of deceit, lies, resentment, and discontentment of heart. Be responsible to yourself, your family, friends, and your obligations. So when do you know it is time to move past the painful emotions in your life? Does that mean that you need to let go completely? Most likely, yes.

Come quickly to Jesus Christ in a time of distress and uncertainty. Come as you are with your mistakes, sorrows, and regrets to the throne of grace and mercy. Avoid brokenness of heart and spirit by seeking the Lord in prayer by resting in the safe hollow of His powerful and protective hand. Should you feel empty and alone, remember He is closer than your breath and knows what you are feeling and thinking before you can even speak. Trust, rest, pray, and worship Him through your tears and heartbreak. Accept His care and provision for your shattered dreams. Pursue the new normal of your life, knowing He will restore His pure light in the cold, ebony darkness that has surrounded you. Call a trusted friend to come alongside to support, love, encourage, and pray with you. Find the joy of the moment. Come as you are with your joys and passions of life. Rest in His hand, and wait for His peace. God lead the Israelites, by day and by night (Exodus 13:21–22), as they journeyed to the Promised Land. He also will faithfully lead on your journey of life.

Shake off the dust of the things that seek to encumber you, and move into His overflowing mercy, grace, love, and forgiveness.

Learn lessons from your life journey and from the men and women of faith you have studied and met along the way. Follow their examples. Their life journeys have modeled for you happy times and sometimes circumstances and environments that were not fun at all! Instead, choose to allow your life to be defined by belief, hope, happiness, contentment, peace, and joy. These character qualities are found in the Lord Jesus Christ, and as you allow Him to take up rightful residence in your life, He will mold these qualities into your character.

He heals the brokenhearted, And binds up their wounds. He counts the number of the stars; He gives names to all of them. Great is our Lord, and abundant in strength; His understanding is infinite. (Psalm 147:3–5)

And the Lord is the one who goes ahead of you; He will be with you. He will not fail you or forsake you. Do not fear, or be dismayed. (Deuteronomy 31:8)

Know you are close to the heart of God! Worship your Lord and Savior, and find your release in Jesus Christ. There are many things you don't understand about tomorrow, but you do know who holds your tomorrow—Jesus Christ!

He found him in a desert land, And in the howling waste of a wilderness; He encircled him, He cared for him, He guarded him as the pupil of His eye. Like an eagle that stirs up its nest, That hovers over its young, He spread His

wings and caught them, He carried them on His pinions.
The Lord alone guided him ... (Deuteronomy 32:10–12a)

It is easy to be defined by positive character attributes when things in your life are going smoothly. When pressure begins to squeeze out what is really inside you, how is your life defined? Life events that toss you into crisis mode will bring about and require change. You will succeed because He is! For God to bring about a change in your life only requires the smallest mustard seed of faith to see it begin to take root inside you. In the good times and in the bad, remember to remain faithful to God. Choose to focus, trust, obey, hope, and follow Him! Remember all the ways the Lord has led you through your wilderness, past, present, and future. He has provided; listen through the stillness and the darkness for and to His instructions. Step out in faith, walk with a grateful heart, and praise and worship Him.

All the ways of a man are clean in his own sight, But the
Lord weighs the motives. Commit your works to the Lord,
and your plans will be established. (Proverbs 16:2–3)

Pursue a life built on godly principles, and follow Him daily. Be obedient and seek His forgiveness. Seek your Father God made known to you through the Lord Jesus Christ. Pray you will make the right choices to ensure your life is defined by Jesus Christ. Throughout the course of your life, you may allow a circumstance, an event, an environment, or a person to irritate you so much that they rob you of your happiness and joy, your energy, and your focus. If you stop and think about it, it is at times like this that you may be the only one suffering. The person who disappointed or angered you most likely has no clue he or she even offended you. And certainly the inanimate object has no idea. You are the one who is miserable, no one else. You are human, and it is hard to let go of hurtful things. Stop replaying the voice of destruction that reminds you of the pain, unfairness, betrayal, disappointment, hurtful words, annoyance, and so on. Leave these circumstances at the throne of grace and mercy in prayer. And don't take them back from Jesus once you have given them to Him. Forgive yourself, love yourself, and be at peace with yourself and your surroundings. Don't beat yourself up by focusing on your own conclusions, which may be right or wrong for the concern at hand. Each day has enough of its own worries; don't create new ones that don't exist.

But the fruit of the Spirit is love, joy, peace, patience, kindness, goodness, faithfulness, gentleness, self-control; against such things there is not law. Now those that belong to Jesus Christ have crucified the flesh with its passions and desires. If we live by the Spirit, let us also walk by the Spirit. Let us not become boastful, challenging one another, envying one another. (Galatians 5:22–26)

So how can you live a life that is defined by God and not your circumstances and environment? Memorize Scripture (or read and reread), and allow God's Word and His promises to permeate your entire being. Meditate on a specific verse or passage, and make it your own. Read the Scripture passage in a different translation of the Bible, diagram the sentence structure of the passage, look up the meaning of the words to understand its meaning more fully. Rewrite the verse(s) in your own words, and put it where you can read it throughout the day. Contemplate what you have read, and ask God to show you how the Scripture applies to your life. Put yourself in the circumstance of the passage—how would you respond, what actions would you take, and so on? By asking God to apply His Word to your life, you will be changed. Pray and seek Christ in all things and at all times. Wrap yourself in the Lord Jesus Christ's marvelous light and love. God comforts you so that you can comfort others.

If I speak with the tongues of men and of angels, but do not have love, I have become a noisy gong or a clanging cymbal. And if I have the gift of prophecy, and know all mysteries and all knowledge; and if I have all faith, so as to remove mountains, but do not have love, I am nothing. And if I give all my possessions to feed the poor, and if I deliver my body to be burned, but do not have love, it profits me nothing. Love is patient, love is kind, and is not jealous; love does not brag and is not arrogant, does not act unbecomingly; it does not seek its own, is not provoked, does not take into account a wrong suffered, does not rejoice in unrighteousness, but rejoices with the truth; bears all things, believes all things, hopes all things, endures all things. Love never fails, (1 Corinthians 13:1–8a)

Even so faith, if it has no works, is dead, being by itself. (James 2:17)

Maybe you have heard the phrase that speaks about walking a mile in another person's shoes before judging another. You come to your life journey with rose colored glasses that have been influenced by your own perspective, interpretation, and outlook on life. Sometimes you are right, and other times you are not. Those around you may be willing to be open to viewing things from your vantage point. And then again, they may not. Love those who hate/irritate/annoy you. Pray for them. Pray the love of God will touch their hearts. Pray that God will use you as a tool of blessing in their lives. Realize unexpected blessings await you as you move forward wrapped securely in the love of God.

I am the true vine, and My Father is the vinedresser. Every branch in Me that does not bear fruit, He takes away; and every branch that bears fruit, He prunes it, that it may bear more fruit. You are already clean because of the word which I have spoken to you. Abide in Me, and I in you. As the branch cannot bear fruit of itself, unless it abides in the vine, so neither can you, unless you abide in Me. I am the vine, you are the branches; he who abides in Me, and I in him, bears much fruit; for apart from Me you can do nothing. If anyone does not abide in Me, he is thrown away as a branch, and dries up; and they gather them, and cast them into the fire, and they are burned. If you abide in Me, and My words abide in you; ask whatever you wish, and it shall be done for you. By this is My Father glorified, that you bear much fruit, and so prove to be My disciples. (John 15:1–8)

Reach out and help others, pray for those experiencing the same or similar circumstances or environments as you. Pray for those who have hurt you; pray for their good, for what makes them happy, for God's blessing to rest upon them, and so on. Take your focus off yourself. Focus on others around you and shake off the dust of darkness. Wrap yourself in the Lord Jesus Christ's marvelous light and love. God comforts you so that you can comfort others. The phrase "pay it forward" is a good one to live by. By being mindful of others, by supporting and encouraging those around you (at home or faraway), and by caring for their needs, lives will be changed, and God's blessing will be experienced. Encouragement and coming alongside another individual or family not only makes a difference in your own life, but it also has an impact in the lives of those you reach out to. You can't earn God's love or earn your salvation, but reaching out to others is always a positive way to move beyond the shadows of the canyons in your life and realize that you are not in the battle alone. And who knows? You may also receive a blessing as well.

Your Heavenly Father is the Most Holy God and your Creator! He is all-powerful, all-knowing, and ever-present in your life and in the lives of those you hold close to your heart. He holds the foundations of the earth and the universe securely in His hand. He is worthy or your trust and worship. He is mighty, and He will deliver you! The Lord alone brings light into your life, and He will bring you out of your darkness. He will fill you with His Holy Spirit, and the light of the Lord Jesus Christ will shine through you. He will use you in your sphere of influence to draw others into a right relationship with His Son. He girds you with strength, trains your hands for good works to build His kingdom, and sets you on your high places. He will unfold circumstances and environments for you that will bring glory to His name. He will uphold you when all seems to be crumbling around you. He acts on your behalf whether you are mindful of it or not! Never forget to praise and worship your Holy and Sovereign God. Thank Him for His mercy and grace and for His extravagant love, care, and provisions. Enjoy the silence of resting in His strong and powerful arms and presence.

Leave the shaken dust of your life at the foot of the cross of Jesus Christ. He is the Master Potter; allow Him to mold you into a new person defined by His forgiveness and love. Christ holds all things together (Colossians 1:17) and makes all things new through His resurrection power. By shaking the dust from your life, you will see the restoration of the peace and joy of your salvation found only in Jesus Christ. And your life will be a light that shines brilliantly, for a great distance, in the darkness and cold silence of a world struggling and seeking to know its Creator God. Learn to listen to the message of God's great love in and through any circumstance or environment of your journey. Being defined by darkness is not who you are called to be. You are called and defined by the pure light of God's love. You are a child of the Most High God. Rejoice and be glad in Him!

Choose this day to follow Him and Him alone. Lord Jesus, give us the strength and courage to love and seek You always, through every season of our lives, until the day You reach out and take our hand to bring us to our eternal home.

The Lord your God is in your midst, A victorious warrior. He will exult over you with joy, He will be quiet in His love, He will rejoice over you with shouts of joy. (Zephaniah 3:17)

A Lesson from a Polar Bear
Contentment–Philippians 4:11
Be at Peace with What the Day Brings Your Way

Watching the polar bear look at the huge expanse of sea ice and knowing it is just beginning the journey to the edges of the Hudson Bay and beyond—on winter terrain—would not be something I would be very peaceful about. Being content in the circumstances the Lord brings our way can be very hard to fathom and live out. It is my prayer that amid your emotions and tears and joys of the day that the Lord God's peace that passes all understanding will engulf you and grant you a calmness the world around you will observe and marvel at. And through your story many individuals will touch the edge of heaven and know He alone is God, and that He saves and makes a difference in your life and theirs today and for all eternity. May you seek to have a living relationship with the Most Holy Creator God and be defined in His love, mercy, and grace for the rest of your days.

Our Journey—Our Faith Story—
Stepping from Darkness in to Light

The Lord lives. Blessed be our Rock, the Lord Jesus Christ! God will be exalted, and we must give thanks and praise to the Lord. Beginning today and for all eternity, as a child of the Redeemer

God, you will be able to worship and praise your Savior and Lord Jesus Christ as you walk your life journey with Him. As your life story is defined, begin now to learn how to seek and worship Christ on a moment-by-moment basis throughout the course of each new day. Praise Him for His great gifts of life and forgiveness. Praise Him for rescuing you from this world of ebony darkness. Praise Him for His restoration and refreshment by defining you as His precious child!

... that at the name of Jesus every knee should bow, of those who are in heaven and on earth, and under the earth, and that every tongue should confess that Jesus Christ is Lord, to the glory of God the Father. (Philippians 2:10–11)

I waited patiently for the Lord; And He inclined to me, and heard my cry. He brought me up out of the pit of destruction, out of the miry clay; And He set my feet upon a rock making my footsteps firm. And He put a new song in my mouth, a song of praise to our God; Many will see and fear. And will trust in the Lord. How blessed is the man who has made the Lord his trust, And has not turned to the proud, nor to those who lapse into falsehood. Many, O Lord my God, are the wonders which Thou hast done, And Thy thoughts towards us; There is none to compare with Thee; If I would declare and speak of them, They would be too numerous to count. (Psalm 40:1–5)

Bless the Lord, O my soul; And all that is within me, bless His holy name. Bless the Lord, O my soul. And forget none of His benefits. (Psalm 103:1–2)

Lord, let Your all-powerful and all-knowing justice break through the darkness and bring us from the silence and cold darkness into the glorious light of Your Son, Jesus Christ! May the Prince of Peace grant you His favor, grace, and mercy. May He enfold you in His love and grant you His perfect peace for now and for all eternity! Let us worship the King of Kings, our Eternal God, forever more, beginning today and throughout all eternity!

Praise the Lord! I will give thanks to the Lord with all my heart, In the company of the upright and in the assembly. Great are the works of the Lord; They are studied by all who delight in them. Splendid and majestic is His work; And His righteousness endures forever. He has made His wonders to be remembered; The Lord is gracious and compassionate. He has given food to those who fear Him; He will remember His covenant forever. He has made known to His people the power of His works, In giving them the heritage of the nations. The works of His hands are truth and justice; All His precepts are sure. They are upheld forever and ever; They are performed in truth and uprightness. He has sent redemption to His people; He has ordained His covenant forever; Holy and awesome is His name. The fear of the Lord is the beginning of wisdom; A good understanding have all those who do His commandments; His praise endures forever. (Psalm 111:1–10)

Selah—Amen!